REVIVING YOUR SEX LIFE AFTER CHILDBIRTH

Your guide to pain-free and pleasurable sex after the baby

By Kathe Wallace, PT, BCB-PMD

Reviving Your Sex Life After Childbirth:

Your Guide to Pain-free and Pleasurable Sex After the Baby

2nd Printing

Address all inquiries and book requests to:

Kathe Wallace, PT, BCB-PMD

Find me on Facebook at:

www.facebook.com/KatheWallacePT and Author

Contact me at:

author@kathewallace.com

www.kathewallace.com

ISBN-13: 978-0-9960298-0-3 (soft cover)

ISBN-13: 978-0-9960298-1-0 (e-book)

Library of Congress Control Number: 2014907532

***Reviving Your Sex Life After Childbirth**, by Kathe Wallace, PT, is a long overdue resource we have been sorely lacking in the field of women's health: an essential expert guide for the almost 4 million women who give birth in the U.S. every year. The postpartum period is a special and wonderful but often stressful phase of life for new mothers, and paying attention to healing, strengthening, and returning to sexual activity gets pushed to the very bottom of most to-do lists. Making matters worse, most new moms receive little formal preparation or information after delivery from their birth attendants, and the normal healing process of the vagina, pelvic floor, and reproductive organs after birth may feel like a mystery to many.*

But now Kathe, in one small book, has filled in this missing piece and brought postpartum women and their medical caregivers forward in leaps and bounds. She explains clearly and in detail, with excellent graphics, many important self-care and strengthening techniques that can hasten healing, stop discomfort, rebuild trust in our amazing pelvic design, improve self-confidence, and enhance pleasure. This knowledge is empowering and may even help women attain a better sex life than before baby.

For women recovering with tears, muscle injury, relaxation symptoms, and other tissue trauma, Kathe applies her expertise in the well established principles of myofascial physiotherapy to guide self treatment of the vulva, vagina, perineum, pelvic girdle, and abdomen, all areas that have to heal well for best body-mind health and function in daily living as well as in sexuality. Obstetricians, midwives, and others in the field of women's health care will greatly benefit from reading this book, and my wish is that they will make it a routine patient education tool for all new moms. Perhaps we can prevent considerable chronic birth related vulvar, pelvic, and sexual pain this way, thanks to Kathe!

March 29, 2014
Deborah Coady, MD, FACOG
Author of Healing Painful Sex: A Woman's Guide to Confronting, Diagnosing, and Treating Painful Sex

DEDICATION

This book is dedicated to all my patients.
Thank you for seeking treatment and encouraging me to share your stories to help all women after childbirth.

ACKNOWLEDGMENTS

I would like to thank many individuals for their help, expertise, inspiration, guidance and support in creating this book.

My first inspiration was from Penny Simkin PT, my personal childbirth educator, whose initial insights into the needs of post-partum women helped me launch my career path in pelvic floor rehabilitation. Her initial comments on the book inspired me to continue to write about my clinical experiences with post-partum women.

My continued inspiration is Holly Herman DPT, OCS, WCS, BCB-PMD, IF, AASECT, PRPC, my esteemed teaching colleague and former business partner. I am grateful to Holly for sharing her extensive knowledge, her unique treatment approaches, her sense of humor, and her joy of teaching.

I am grateful for the constant encouragement from Deanna Spada, Darrell Gantt and Joseph Spada. It is a delight to share a vision and have your ongoing support.

There are many professionals who advised me along the way. These include physical therapists Dawn Sandalcidi, PT, RCMT, BCB-PMD, Beth Swanson, MS, PT, OCS, ATC, Diane Lee, BSR, FACMPT, CGIMS, Ramona Horton, MPT, Tracy Sher, MPT, CSCS and doctors Heather S. Howard, PhD, MPH, Arnold I. Levin, MD, Karny Jacoby,

MD, Gina Lagalbo, MD, and Barbara Levy, MD. I was also fortunate to work with independent study students from the University of Washington, Division of Physical Therapy, Katie McGee, Megan Fisher, Sarah Plumer-Holzman, Natalie Freis, Sarah Elizabeth Benditt, and Lindsy B. Campbell. Thank you all for your research, review, and contributions to the text.

I also appreciate the editing skills of Roxanne Richardson, Rosalee Gamella and Helen Dailey-Fallat. Graphic artist Emilie McIntyre was extremely helpful and patient with the development and revisions of the illustrations throughout the book.

I also thank all my patients and their partners (whose names are confidential). Many of them offered to read the first drafts of my book, contributed the stories, and encouraged this book to completion.

And to my son, Jake, whose spirit and love is a continual joy to me.

MEDICAL DISCLAIMER

The medical information contained in this book is for informational and educational purposes only. This book is not intended to replace professional medical advice, diagnosis, or treatment. This book is not designed to replace a physician's judgment about the appropriateness or risks of a technique or therapy for a given patient. Nothing contained in this book constitutes a professional diagnosis, treatment, or patient therapist relationship.

Readers should seek the advice of a physician, women's health provider, and/or a qualified therapist with any questions regarding specific medical conditions and treatment. Neither the author nor the publisher is liable for any injuries or other incidents arising out of acts in reliance on the information contained in this book. Readers who fail to consult appropriate medical professionals, delay seeking medical advice, disregard medical advice, or discontinue medical treatment because of information contained in this book assume the risk of injury. If you think you may be suffering from a medical condition, obtain immediate medical attention.

The publisher is not responsible for errors or omissions in the content of this book. The author and publisher welcome any reader to report to the publisher any discrepancies or inaccuracies noticed in the text.

CONTENTS

INTRODUCTION

The Common Story: Emily

My first time having sex post-partum was extremely painful. During penetration and after, I felt a tight, sharp, steady pain that lasted up to three hours. My pain rating was high; if 10 was the most intolerable, it felt like an 8. Thinking this was a temporary side effect from having a baby, I waited it out, but quickly found I was avoiding having sex altogether. After two months, I saw my health care provider about this issue. I felt so discouraged when she told me she had never heard of a problem like this without having an episiotomy. After hearing this from a 30-year veteran of childbirth, I was painfully discouraged and blamed myself. I kept avoiding sex and became defensive and tearful whenever my husband brought up the topic of our sex life. After seven months, a friend of mine suggested I pursue pelvic physical therapy (PT).

The first benefit I gained from pelvic PT was to hear that many women have experienced the same thing. This was such a relief, that tears came to my eyes. Why did no one talk about this effect?! Through the next several sessions of PT there were several key skills and bits of education that ultimately led to my successful treatment.

First, the use of biofeedback allowed me to "get to know" the tension in my pelvic floor. I had been keeping those muscles in constant contraction. Turns out I hold stress in more places than my back and shoulders. Daily practice in releasing and relaxing my pelvic floor was critical. I learned how to control that part of my body and stay present to what it was telling me. Second, manual massage of the scar tissue from my tear allowed it to loosen and also helped me practice relaxing my pelvic floor with penetration. After several weeks, I was ready to try intercourse and felt pretty confident. Mentally, I was armed with some helpful information from my PT sessions, which ultimately helped me achieve orgasm for the first time, post-partum. I was taught that I could actually move my clitoris using my pelvic floor muscles. Knowing how to use your pelvic floor muscles to enhance intercourse is something I highly recommend. "Getting to know" my pelvic floor has allowed me to enjoy sex once again and read my body on a whole new level

After childbirth, your body requires care and healing in the area that carried the largest load—your pelvic floor and pelvic girdle. It is common for almost every woman to have discomfort for a few weeks, and half of women who deliver vaginally have some discomfort for at least three months after childbirth. As a new mother, you can have pain or muscle weakness, which can cause changes in sensation or support around the vagina. Also, you can experience problems with sexual intercourse or physical contact within the pelvis region and abdominal wall.

This discomfort is treatable, and medical evidence indicates that **you can reclaim your previous sex life.** Changes to the pelvic girdle and pelvic floor can affect your ability to do simple daily tasks as well as your overall sense of sexuality and self-image. Fortunately, there is help available to address these changes. **If your recovery is painful in your genital region and you miss your "old" body, there is a program that will help you.**

Let's face it: most of the post-delivery attention is placed on your infant. It is up to you to take charge of your body. In the United States, post-delivery hospital stays are shorter today than ever before—about one to two days after a vaginal birth and three days after a cesarean. New moms have little personal recovery time before they are sent home to care for an infant. On the contrary, this book is for you, the mom! It describes post-partum care especially directed to your pelvic floor muscles and your vaginal tissues.

The old-fashioned way is to assume that persistent perineal pain after delivery is normal. Often a new mom doesn't mention to her doctor during her post-partum visit that she is experiencing vaginal or genital pain at rest, with activity, or during the exam. Why? Because she thinks this pain is normal. Often times, if she does report to her health care provider that she is experiencing discomfort (and her exam is negative for infection or poor tissue healing), her health care provider will likely suggest baseline measures such as relaxation and perhaps the use of lubrication. Sometimes a surgical option is offered, but she may be told she is "too young for surgery on her organs" and not offered any alternatives for dealing with pelvic discomfort. However, there is a growing specialty in physical therapy focusing on women's health and the pelvic floor muscles. This specialty offers evaluation and treatment of post-partum women with the goal of complete recovery from musculoskeletal and sexual pain. The evaluation includes assessing the pelvic floor muscles for spasm or weakness and identifying painful regions in the muscles and genital skin that might not move well after birth. Physical therapists can also use a biofeedback machine that helps you see your ability to release or contract the pelvic floor muscles.

Women's health pelvic physical therapists are trained to assess the body as a whole with an emphasis on the impact of the musculoskeletal system on bladder, bowel, and sexual function.

These therapists have gone beyond entry-level training and taken continuing education classes to learn specific pelvic floor muscle examination techniques and to study sexual, urologic/gynecologic, colorectal, neurologic, and dermatologic conditions. All these conditions can impact an individual's function and movement. To find a physical therapist in the United States, visit womenshealthapta.org/pt-locator/ or visit hermanwallace.com/practitioner-directory. The interest and expertise of this type of therapy spans the world. The International Organization of Physical Therapists in Women's Health (IOPTWH) has a mission to improve health care for women internationally through facilitation and promotion of best-practice women's health physical therapy. Their website at IOPTWH.org will link you to 23 countries that have women's health/pelvic groups.

For more than 25 years I have dedicated my physical therapy practice to women's health and pelvic floor physical therapy. In the medically progressive Pacific Northwest, if a new mother reports problems with her vagina or pelvis, her doctor or midwife often refers her to me or other physical therapists who specialize in women's health or pelvic floor physical therapy. There are solutions to these little discussed but specific health concerns!

I wrote this book because my patients are surprised when I discuss the available treatment, education, exercise, and manual techniques to facilitate normal function of the pelvic floor and genital tissues after childbirth. They often ask, "Why didn't anyone tell me?" This book will help spread the word to women who might otherwise not find out. In this book, I present information on how to restore your pelvic floor sensations and tone, and prepare your body to return to an active sexual life. This book contains practical instructions on what to do if it hurts before you start, when you start, or after you are done with sexual activity.

All these instructions are described so you can help yourself learn more about your body and simple techniques to restore and revive it after childbirth. Although this information is designed as a woman's manual for self-care that does not mean that you should not involve your partner along the way. Sometimes you might prefer to be independent and do the techniques privately; other times you may rather have the company of your partner, or may in fact need their help with the techniques.

Your sexual desire may take on different patterns with the addition of a child. First, let's acknowledge that returning to sexual activity after having a baby is a challenge for many couples. It is an exhausting experience to juggle the 24/7 needs of a newborn. The experience can be overwhelming until there is a developed routine for you, your partner, and your baby. Having an interest in sexual activity can wax and wane throughout your recovery. As your bond develops with your new baby, you may be less available emotionally for healthy sexual activity. On the other hand, you may find this bond enhances intimacy and can intensify romantic feelings for your partner.

Women have a wide range of sexual desires after childbirth. You may have no sexual interest because you are experiencing persistent vaginal and genital discomfort, vaginal discharge, or dryness. Your desire to be sexual may be accompanied by emotions and fears about how your post-partum body works, how it performs, and how your partner sees your body. Psychosocial influences such as post-partum depression or specific religious or cultural practices may influence your timing on returning to sexual activity. Pregnancy may also be a concern, so be sure to discuss birth control with your partner and your health care provider. I am writing this book because when the sexual desire is present, but accompanied with discomfort, it is hard to not give up your sex life altogether. I encourage you to reunite with your sexual self and the intimacy that it brings to your relationship if that is your desire.

Commit to discussing your sexual desires and fears with your partner. It is important to share with your partner the changes you are experiencing in your body after childbirth. Changes take place all over your body, but least understood by most are the physical changes around and in the vagina and pelvic floor muscles. The vagina can feel weak and stretched out from a vaginal delivery. It is very common to have a dry vagina because of a decrease in estrogen after delivery. If your perineum tore or you had an episiotomy, the incision or scar around the vagina may be tight and painful. The stiched area can hurt even after it is healed. Your vagina can also feel loose and have less sensation. Your abdomen and belly may have low tone and feel flabby. You may experience less bladder or bowel control. These are not changes that you want to share with the world, but sharing your concerns or fears with your partner is important.

Most doctors and midwives recommend that you wait six weeks after childbirth before resuming vaginal penetration or intercourse. This waiting period typically ends at your six-week post-partum visit with the doctor or midwife. At that time your health care provider routinely examines the vaginal region for tissue healing. Even if you are feeling ready, it usually takes a minimum of four weeks for the tissues around and in the vagina, known as the perineum, to recover from a vaginal birth. When you have an episiotomy, a vaginal tear (a common response to excessive stretching), or a more difficult delivery with the use of a vacuum or forceps, you may need to wait longer than six weeks. Research shows that women who had tears, that go to or through the anus (called third- and fourth-degree lacerations), usually have some temporary difficulty with resuming intercourse and experience more discomfort. All types of deliveries can adversely affect the vaginal canal, the entrance, and its sensation. If you do not feel ready to resume any type of sexual activity, give yourself a break, but be sure to express your desires and feelings to your partner. You do not need to start with intercourse. If however you are feeling ready before your six-week check please check with your doctor or midwife before resuming intercourse. Be aware that the typical "green light" requirements for resuming sexual activity are vulvar and perineal tissue healing, and the availability and use of contraception. Expect that there may be some initial pain when the tissues stretch or are touched, but it should not be excessive or persistent. This should lessen with each attempt at sexual activity. If the pain does not lessen or becomes worse, it is important to make an appointment with your health care provider.

Sometimes tissue healing is delayed because of stretching, severity of the tearing, the type of sutures used, your hormonal changes, and smoking habits. Your doctor can assess if there is a problem that requires medical intervention such as a fissure, fistula, or hemorrhoids. In addition, many women have low estrogen levels after childbirth and especially while breastfeeding, which causes the vaginal walls to become temporarily dry and delicate. Any genital or vaginal touch would then become more painful than pleasurable. If you experience these symptoms, your practitioner will be able to decide if you are a candidate for treatment or perhaps temporary medications that can help the condition.

Please see your doctor if you are having persistent pain at the episiotomy or tear site, painful vaginal penetration, or are unable to have intercourse. Do not delay; it is not normal for this pain to persist. Touch and sexual experiences should be pleasurable not painful. I encourage you to ask questions of your health care provider and not to be afraid of getting a second opinion.

The following 10 tips and guidelines address the needs of all post-partum women who are struggling with changes in their body after having a baby. This book contains important education, exercises, and activities designed to help you return to an active sex life that includes touching the genital tissues and vaginal penetration. The first two sections in this book review the anatomy of the vulva and perineal area and teach you how to do a general scan of your vulvar region and muscles so that you can do an assessment of your body. The remainder of the book provides activities that address problems with discomfort or persistent pain by providing instructions to minimize the pain caused by a lack of mobility, weakness, and muscle tension. Also included are breathing activities for pain relief and sexual arousal. Though each woman is unique in her recovery, every woman can benefit from the education, exercises, and activities in this book to help her enjoy an active and satisfying sex life that includes intercourse or vaginal penetration after childbirth. If intercourse is not your goal, but you are experiencing persistent discomfort in the genital region, these tips can help you as well.

GLOSSARY

Glossary of Anatomical Terms/Conditions

GENERAL REGION

Perineum: The external region at the base of the pelvis between the sitting bones, pubic bone, and tailbone; includes the orifices (openings) of the bladder, rectum, and vagina as well as muscles, organs, glands, and structurally supportive skin and fascia. It forms a diamond shape between the pubic bone and tailbone and the two sitting bones.

Figure 1 • The Perineum Basic Parts

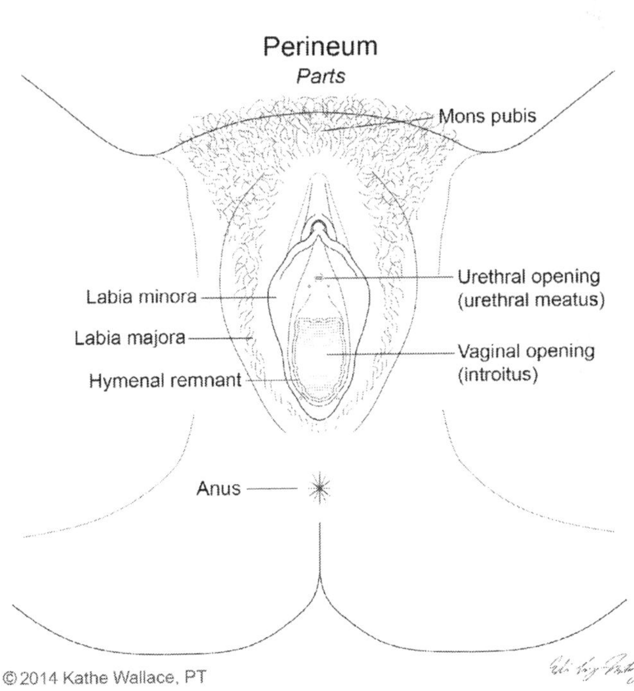

ANATOMICAL REGIONS WITHIN THE PERINEUM

Perineal body: The junction where muscles and fascia join between the vagina and anus. It is also a connecting point of the surface and deep muscles of the pelvic floor. This is where many of the pelvic floor muscles attach. The perineal body region may be cut in an episiotomy or can be torn during delivery. It is sometimes called the central tendon of the perineum.

Vulva: The area of the perineum from the perineal body to the mons pubis. This includes the outer visible parts include the labia majora and minora, clitoris, urinary opening, vaginal opening, and perineal body. This region is also often called the genitals or genitalia.

Vestibule: An oval-shaped area located inside the labia minora; this area contains the introitus (the vaginal opening), vestibular glands, and the urethral meatus (the urinary opening).

Posterior fourchette: An area of mucosal skin that is located opposite from the clitoris at the inferior (bottom) part of the vaginal opening. This skin is often stretched during intercourse or torn with vaginal delivery.

PARTS OF THE PERINEUM

Labia majora: The fleshy, cushioning outer lips near the vagina that are covered with pubic hair.

Labia minora: The inner lips, or flaps, which are thinner and can be more pigmented; they join at the clitoris.

Mons pubis: Fat pad with hair over the pubic bone.

Introitus: The term for the opening of the vagina; the vagina is a canal that connects the uterus (womb) to the perineum.

Hymenal remnant: The residual membrane that once covered the vaginal opening (introitus).

Anus: The rectal opening that is the outlet for bowel movements.

Urethral meatus: The term for the urinary opening where urine empties from the bladder; the urethra is the tube that connects the urinary bladder to the perineum.

Figure 2 • The Perineum with Vulvar Detail

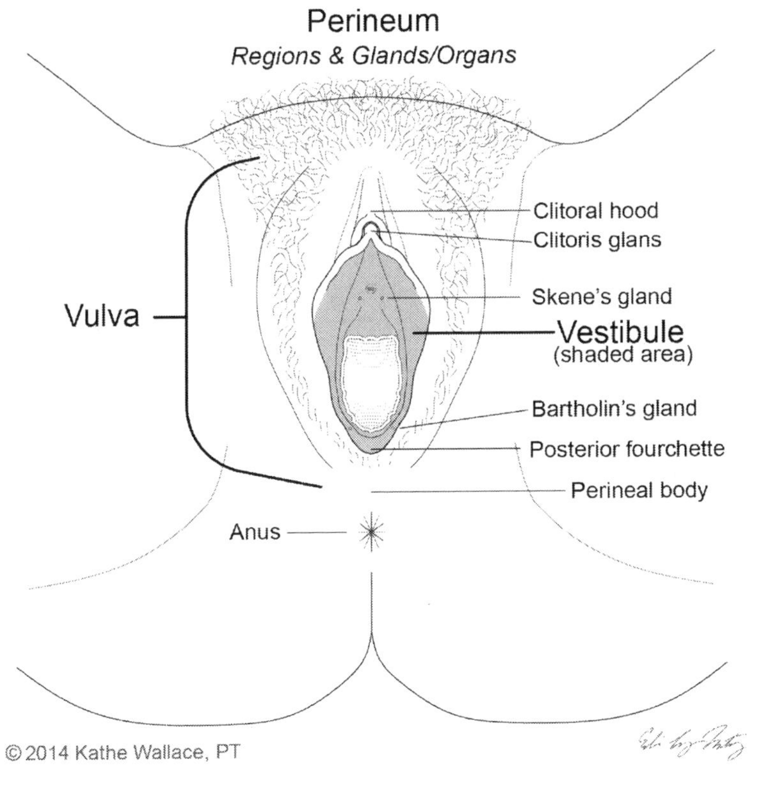

Perineum
Regions & Glands/Organs
Clitoral hood
Clitoris glans
Skene's gland
Vulva
Vestibule
(shaded area)
Bartholin's gland
Posterior fourchette
Perineal body
Anus
©2014 Kathe Wallace, PT

GLANDS/ORGANS

Skene's gland: Located on the anterior (top) wall of the vagina near the opening of the urethra, this gland secretes a lubricating fluid during arousal and is responsible for secreting female ejaculate, usually when stimulated directly. This gland is part of the G-spot region of the vagina. It is sometimes called the lesser vestibular gland or the female prostate.

Bartholin's gland: Located between muscles of the pelvic floor, this gland provides lubrication for the vagina. It is sometimes called the greater vestibular gland.

Clitoris: The erectile female organ (equivalent to the male penis) that is responsive to sexual stimulation. The clitoris is shaped like a wishbone and it has three main parts. All parts are sexually sensitive.

1. ***Glans Clitoris:*** the head or external portion of clitoris.
2. ***Clitoral Hood:*** a protective skin over the glans called the prepuce.
3. ***Crus of Clitoris:*** the "leg-like" extensions of the clitoris that connect from the glans to the vulvar region on each side of the vagina.

PELVIC FLOOR MUSCLES

The pelvic floor consists of multiple muscles comprised in three layers. The side view in Figure 3 shows the surface layers (one and two) and the deep layer (three). This group of muscles is commonly called the Kegel muscles. They were named after an American doctor who promoted pelvic floor muscle strengthening for treatment of poor tone and function of the genital muscles, urinary stress incontinence, and improvement of sexual function. In some cases these muscles need to be strengthened, yet in other cases they need to be stretched and released. See Tips 5, 7, 8, and 9 for more information on how the muscles work.

Figure 3 • Side View of Pelvic Floor Muscles and Organs

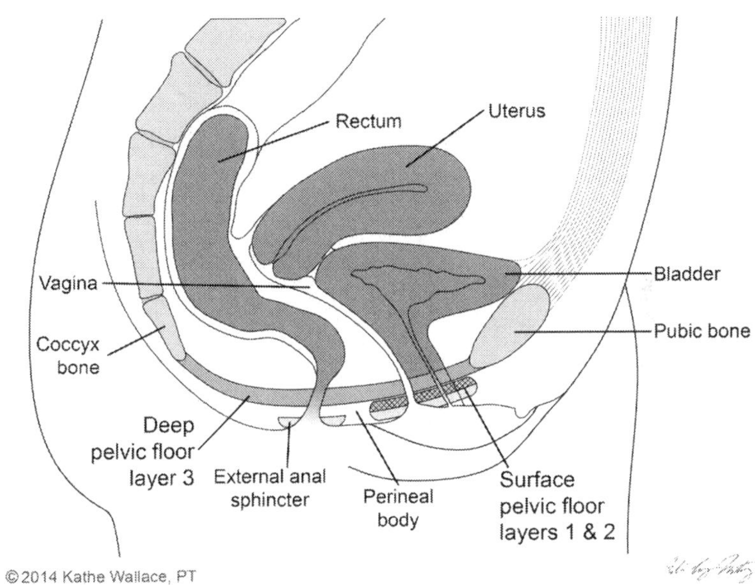

SURFACE MUSCLES: PELVIC FLOOR LAYERS 1 AND 2

Both these muscle layers surround the outlets of the perineum. These muscles are sphincters that close off or open the outlets of the bladder, bowel, and vagina. There are two muscles in the first layer that attach to and can move the clitoris.

DEEP MUSCLES: LAYER 3

This layer includes muscles that form a floor in the pelvis as they sling from the pubic bone to the tailbone. These muscles support the vagina and internal organs in their proper position and can tighten the vaginal and rectal canals when contracted. The muscles in this layer are usually the ones women consider as their entire pelvic floor, but in fact this is only one portion of the muscle group. They are known as the levator ani muscles. For more detailed information about the pelvic floor muscles see the Appendix.

OTHER TERMS AND CONDITIONS

Fascia: Fascia is connective tissue below the skin present throughout the body. It can be dense or loose and located between or around muscles, bones, or organs, where it connects and sometimes wraps around muscles, organs, nerves, bones, and vessels of the body.

Episiotomy: The term for a cut between the vagina and the anus in the perineal body region. It is performed by the health care provider when a delivery needs to happen quickly, the child is in an abnormal position, or the health care provider feels that extensive tearing is likely to occur during vaginal delivery. Recovery can be uncomfortable and be a cause of painful vaginal penetration for months after delivery.

Lochia: Lochia is a normal discharge from the uterus coming out of the birth canal (vagina) that occurs while the uterus is recovering from delivery. It has an odor similar to your menstrual flow. Typically the flow changes color and diminishes in volume from bloody to yellowish-white over the course of several weeks.

OVERVIEW: HOW CHILDBIRTH CHANGES YOUR BODY AND CHALLENGES YOUR SEXUALITY. WHAT HAPPENS TO MAKE IT CHANGE?

Many of my clients ask what happens "down there" with delivery. No two deliveries are alike, but the types of problems women experience that will benefit from self-care can be simply divided into two categories. The first type of problem is restricted mobility of the vaginal and vulvar tissues. This restriction in perineal and vaginal mobility can be present with or without muscle spasm. The muscle spasm or trigger point is a response to pain, stitches, and overstretching in the vaginal area. The second type of problem is weakness and laxity from stretching of muscle, fascia, and ligaments. During a vaginal delivery the pelvic floor muscles, fascia, and ligaments can stretch and sometimes tear. Both types of problems can cause pain during intercourse, penetration, or even just touch on or around your genitals. Detailed descriptions of these two categories of problems that can benefit from the specific techniques in this book are further described to help you understand your body changes after delivery.

Problem #1: *Pain and Restricted Mobility from Tears or Episiotomy*

Every birth is different and the passage of the baby through the birth canal can cause damage to the internal vaginal walls as well as to the external perineum. Perineal tears or lacerations are the consequence of some vaginal births. This is more common with difficult births including the use of a vacuum or forceps to assist in delivery. When there is assistance needed for childbirth, an episiotomy is usually performed. These changes can cause restricted mobility and pain when touched or moved. These tears can make it difficult for you to walk, and cause other problems in your everyday activities.

Internal damage to the vaginal walls and the muscles and fascia can be obscure and less obvious to notice post-delivery. Sometimes there are abrasions to the vaginal tissues that can be painful, but usually resolve within the first six weeks after delivery. Some vaginal wall tearing requires stitching and repair immediately after birth. More significant internal tears can cause separation of the muscles from the fascia that support pelvic organs. This separation can be painful, but the typical symptom is feeling loose or weak, as if your organs are falling out of your body. This is called prolapse.

The severity of the changes to the external tissues with the laceration or tear is given a rating (degree), with a higher number representing more tearing or changes to the perineum. Table One outlines the laceration degree scale that is used by medical professionals. These terms are more common, as women are often told about the degree of laceration or tearing they had with delivery.

Any type of external tear or laceration can restrict your ability to move freely. Working to stretch out and release any restrictions is usually the first step. (See Tips 4, 6, and 7.) Trying to strengthen a tight, restricted muscle usually leads to more discomfort and is a common mistake I see women make when they are trying to fix the problem of pain with intercourse without guidance. When muscles and skin have good mobility, strengthening exercises should not be painful. It is an important step to take a personal inventory of your perineum and vagina (see Tip 2) before beginning intercourse or any activities in this book.

Table One: External Perineal Lacerations

DEGREE	AREAS AFFECTED
First Degree	Skin and mucous membrane around the vagina
Second Degree	Skin, mucous membrane around the vagina, the connective tissue between the vagina and the rectum and first two layers of muscles. An episiotomy is a second-degree surgical laceration.
Third Degree	Skin, mucous membrane around the vagina, the connective tissue between the vagina and the rectum and deep layers of muscles. There is a partial tear of the anal sphincter.
Fourth Degree	Skin, mucous membrane of the vagina perineal muscles, perineal body, muscles of the anus and anterior rectal wall, tear of the internal anal sphincter and rectal mucosa. This means there is a tear from the vagina all the way to the anus.

PELVIC FLOOR MUSCLE KNOTS, SPASMS, OR TRIGGER POINTS

A prolonged pushing phase of labor or a difficult delivery increases the risk for muscle knots/spasms or trigger points in the pelvic region. Trauma or injury to the pelvic floor muscles can also lead to the development of a trigger point. A trigger point is an area that can cause persistent pain and limitation of muscle motion. It is commonly described as a taut band or knot in a muscle that, when touched, refers pain to the local area or even to an area far away from the muscle trigger point. Conscious or unconscious contraction of the pelvic floor muscles can also cause trigger points. Muscle knots/spasms and trigger points are all possible to get in the last trimester of pregnancy or during delivery. Trigger points respond best to direct pressure and stretching (see Tips 4, 5, 6, and 7) techniques discussed in this book.

Problem #2: *Pelvic Floor Muscle Weakness and Laxity*

Stretching of muscles, fascia, and nerves occurs with most vaginal births. This can cause a decrease in strength of the pelvic floor muscles. Even if your pelvic floor muscles are strong, childbirth can cause stretching and laxity of the supportive fascia. This laxity can cause a feeling of pelvic heaviness and a sensation that your organs are falling out. This also can contribute to changes in bladder and bowel control.

Problems with bladder and bowel control should not be present once your perineum heals. Muscles that are too loose or stretched out are unable to generate a muscle contraction that completely supports the internal organs. Tears in the muscles will alter the strength and sensation in the vagina or might cause bladder leakage and bowel control problems. If you leak urine when you sneeze, cough, laugh, or lift something, or lose stool when you have an urge for a bowel movement or soil your underwear on the way to the toilet, see your health care provider and talk about these problems. They are more common than you would imagine and help is available. Doing the pelvic floor strengthening exercises in this book is one of the first steps to recovering bladder and bowel control.

Some post-partum women report a sensation that something is falling out of their vagina. They likely are experiencing pelvic organ prolapse (POP), which is simply called "prolapse." Prolapse is a structural change that can occur in the position of the bladder, rectum, or uterus after delivery causing a protrusion into or out of the vaginal canal. These changes occur when the pelvic muscle and fascia support is stretched or sometimes torn. According to the primary medical research reviews of the Cochrane Library, 50% of women who have had children have some degree of prolapse. Some prolapse can be present without causing symptoms. Symptoms are usually felt in the vagina causing a bulge or feeling of fullness. They say that tampons don't fit the same or the urine spray feels changed. Many women also feel loose, with a lack of support in the vagina and perineal area. The sensation is usually worsened with lifting, straining, coughing, sneezing, or with prolonged standing or carrying a child.

When the main area affected is related to the urethra region or front of the vaginal wall, structural changes can cause you to dribble urine on the toilet seat after you urinate, or make it feel like your urine stream has changed angles or sprays differently. Urine leakage with activity can also occur. This leakage with activity is called stress urinary incontinence. If a prolapse is very severe, it can sometimes slow your urine flow.

When the main area affected is related to the rectum, structural changes can cause difficulty emptying the bowels, or it feels like you have an incomplete bowel movement. It is common for women to report that they have to push and support the area around the rectum in order to empty out a bowel movement. This supportive pressure is known as splinting. If they do not do this technique to support the perineum, the stool gets stuck and they can't have a bowel movement.

Prolapse can also be the cause of painful intercourse. When ligaments, fascia, and muscles get stretched or sometimes torn, the organs do not stay in their normal position and women experience discomfort with vaginal penetration, including sexual intercourse. They may also experience pressure in the low back and belly, or heaviness in the pelvis that worsens with sexual activity. No matter how the symptoms present, they not only affect a women's ability to perform daily activities, but also her self-image. Strengthening exercises for the pelvic floor may prevent prolapse from getting worse (see Tip 8) and when done correctly and consistently, can help correct the pelvic organ prolapse by one stage (see Table 2).

Below are some common terms used by doctors, nurses, or midwives to describe prolapse.

Prolapse: A general term used to describe the change of an organ position. The rectum, uterus, bladder, or urethra can change position and be felt in the vagina as a bulge or heaviness.

Cystocele: A condition where the bladder drops and pushes on the top (anterior) wall of the vagina. It is sometimes called anterior wall relaxation.

Rectocele: A condition where the rectum drops and pushes on the back (posterior) wall of the vagina. It is sometimes called posterior wall relaxation.

Some women discover these changes after a long day of physical activity or with a specific event, like lifting a heavy suitcase or box. These bulges sometimes only appear after a cough or while lifting your child out of a crib. Sometimes they are present without straining. What they are feeling is a herniation, or weakening of the vaginal wall.

Prolapse is usually measured by your health care provider by asking a woman to strain maximally while they observe the effect of the strain. The health care provider can measure the amount of prolapse and stage it by how far it is coming out of the vagina. When observed vaginally, the descent of the organs is either above or below the hymenal remnant.

TABLE TWO: STAGES OF PROLAPSE OBSERVED IN THE VAGINA

STAGE	AMOUNT OF DESCENT FRONT OR BACK
0	There is no descent of the vaginal walls
1	Descent is above the hymen by 1 cm or more
2	Descent is between 1 cm above the hymen and 1cm below the hymen
3	Descent is 1 cm to 2 cm below the hymen
4	Descent is greater than 2 cm past the hymen

When organs descend more than 1 cm below the hymen, women report it usually feels like the organs are out of the body. This condition can be treated with pelvic floor strengthening exercises and postural and behavioral changes. Pelvic floor muscle strength and endurance exercises help build the muscles that support the organs and can minimize the symptoms of prolapse. Another non-surgical treatment is with a pessary. A pessary is a supportive device for the internal organs that is placed in the vagina (like a tampon or diaphragm for birth control) and supports the internal organs like a bra supports the breasts. Some women report that it is easier to do pelvic floor exercise when the organs are supported in the correct place by a pessary. They also report a relief of falling-out symptoms. Pessaries are taken out during sexual intercourse and do require special care and the dexterity to place and remove them in the vagina. Pessaries are fitted by your obstetrician, gynecologist, urogynecologist or a health care practitioner.

SOME MORE THINGS THAT CAN HAPPEN WITH CHILDBIRTH

Pregnancy and childbirth can increase your risk for hemorrhoids. Larger infants, pushing a long time, straining with labor, or a traumatic birth can all increase your risk of developing these enlarged or swollen veins in or around the anus. Hemorrhoids occur when there are changes in the veins that supply the anus and the lower rectum. The swelling of the veins can be present around the outside of the anus or can be inside, out of view. This swelling sometimes makes sitting and bowel movements painful, and can cause rectal bleeding or itching. Performing a sitz bath (see Tip 1) and following good perineal care guidelines (see Tip 1) can be the first step to relieving symptoms. Be sure to keep your stools soft and regular and take the suggested medications after delivery until you are pain free. Generally hemorrhoids will resolve in six weeks.

After delivery, one condition that can occur for the first time or with greater frequency is air passing from the vaginal canal. This may be referred to as "queefing" or "varting." It can occur in women who have not had children, but can more frequently be present after vaginal delivery. It is not uncommon in women who have not had children, but can often begin to occur or increase after vaginal delivery. Most women are very embarrassed from this sound that comes from their vagina and mimics the escape of gas from the rectum. "Queefing" may happen with increased frequency after delivery when a woman changes position from sit to stand, performs a yoga pose, or is sexually active. This noise is not a signal of harm to your body but may be a consequence of overstretched muscles and fascia. The good news it there is no odor associated with this noise. If there is a fecal odor, this can be a sign of a serious problem such as a rectal vaginal fistula, and you should discuss this with your health care provider immediately.

A fissure is an abrasion, crack, or tear appearing on or in the vagina and its opening. The most common reasons for fissures are vaginal childbirth and vaginal penetration with excessive stretching. Many women may have experienced a fissure before childbirth when they have sexual intercourse with a partner who has a large penis or perform vigorous intercourse especially when there is dryness or lack of vaginal lubrication. This usually heals spontaneously. A common area for the fissure is the posterior fourchette. What is less often discovered are internal fissures with vaginal birth, sometimes referred to as "skid marks," produced as the baby leaves the vaginal canal. Internal vaginal changes are difficult to evaluate immediately after delivery, so if problems persist, seeing your health care provider post-partum is important.

A fistula is an abnormal opening or passage between organs. With a fistula, an abnormal passage forms between your internal organs, such as the rectum, vagina, and bladder. It can happen with the trauma of childbirth and not be immediately recognized. Symptoms produce pain and "nightmare" symptoms such as fecal matter or urine exiting through the vagina. These are typically repaired surgically to restore normal function.

Changes to your abdominal (belly) strength occur from the growth of the baby stretching the muscles. This causes weakness and sometimes a split in the muscles down the front of the abdominal wall. This split is known as a diastasis rectus abdominis (DRA) and is discussed in Tip 10. The belly often has stretch marks from several months of progressive stretch. The abdominal wall is one of the key muscle groups in post-partum recovery when laxity and weakness are contributing to the problem.

Now let's start with the tips. Here are some specifics on what you can do to understand your body and help you recover from childbirth.

TIP 1: WASH, WEAR, AND CARE—YOUR PERINEUM AFTER BIRTH AND BEYOND

"Ouch! How do I take care of this body part?"

In the early phase of post-partum recovery, pain and discomfort of the perineum are common. You'll want the entire pelvic area to heal rapidly and to feel good when you return to sexual activity. Whether you had a small tear, stretched skin, or an incision for an episiotomy during labor, the skin and the muscles around the vagina need a special attention program. Practicing these self-care tips will help you heal with minimal discomfort. These self-care strategies are also good to practice when needed to maintain a healthy perineum for a lifetime.

INITIAL POST-PARTUM CARE FOR THE GENITAL/VULVAR REGION

In the first six weeks after delivery, your uterus returns to its non-pregnant size. During this time, your uterus produces a discharge called lochia. Many women are extremely self-conscious about how their vagina looks and how lochia smells after delivery. However, there is a normal smell of lochia and over-washing your perineum and vagina can actually lead to an overgrowth of abnormal bacteria. This means that rubbing and scrubbing not only feels awful but is also damaging to the tender skin. The vagina was designed to be self-cleaning, so be gentle and only use water to wash. If you wear pads, panty hose, and tight clothing for long periods of time, you may notice skin irritation or get a yeast infection. Wear pads that do not irritate the skin, and be sure to change them often to let the skin breathe. To minimize irritation, use cotton menstrual flow pads rather than panty liners as they are less irritating to your skin. Wear cotton underwear and consider going without underwear for periods of time when possible.

IMPROVING CIRCULATION: SITZ BATH

Improved circulation and relaxation of the perineal area are facilitated by using a cool or warm water sitz bath starting as soon as 12 hours after childbirth. A sitz bath is done by soaking the perineum in water to clean and soothe the tissues. It is also commonly used for early hemorrhoid care after delivery. You may have taken a sitz bath in the hospital post-delivery, and you can continue these baths at home. It is quicker and more efficient than taking a regular bath. It is also a good way to practice vulvar hygiene for a lifetime. You will need a sitz bath basin (available commercially) that you suspend over the toilet opening. Fill the basin with enough warm or cool water so that your perineum can soak. Take time to relax and get the full benefit. This can be your 10-20 minute solitude break. After the bath, be sure to **pat**, not rub, the perineum dry. Or you may prefer to use a hair dryer on a low heat or cool setting to minimize irritation. Hold the dryer eight inches away and move it back and forth just a few times so that you do not over-dry the area.

CLEANSING THE AREA:

Vulvar skin is sensitive and needs special cleansing care. These tips will minimize irritation of the vulvar area.

The vulvar area can be cleansed after urination or a bowel movement using a squeezable bottle (peri bottle). Use only water in the bottle. Point it so that you squirt water from front to back (toward the anus). Avoid getting shampoo or soap of any kind on the vulvar region, and consider using natural or gentle, fragrance free cleansers. It is not recommended to scrub the vulvar area or douche the vagina. Always clean and pat dry in the direction of front to back toward your anus to avoid wiping any remaining feces onto your healing tissues and perineal body and to prevent urinary tract infections. Usually patting with soft gauze in the early post-delivery days is recommended. If touching the area is too tender, you may use a hair dryer at a cool setting for a short period of time.

EASING THE SORENESS: APPLYING COLD AND HOT COMPRESSES

Swelling in the perineum is common, and applying cold and hot compresses can be quite soothing. For the first 48-hour time period after delivery apply cold compresses to help with swelling. Crushed ice works better than ice cubes, but both can be messier than gel packs available at the drug store. You may keep an individual commercial gel pack or a dedicated bag of frozen corn or peas in the freezer for applying cold to the perineum. Wrap the bag or pack in a towel to protect your skin from direct cold and apply the bag on the perineum for 10–20 minutes. After the first 48 hours, try switching to heat. A heating pad or an old-fashioned water bottle can be soothing. Again, use a cotton towel or cloth between your skin and the heat. Use the heat for 10–20 minutes at a time. Alternating cold and hot can also be beneficial, especially if there is a lot of swelling. Try cold for five minutes, then heat for five minutes, alternating two times for a total of 20 minutes.

EASING THE SORENESS: SETTING UP A SITTING STATION

It usually feels best to have no pressure on your perineal area, so devote one or two areas in your home as sitting stations for feeding and self-care. Create a stable sitting surface by placing cushions under each thigh or sit bone to create a space so no weight bearing occurs on the painful area. With the cushions, sit evenly on the chair or surface with your feet flat on the floor, and avoid leaning too much to one side, which could cause the stitches to pull or make your back hurt from the twisted posture. Doughnut-shaped cushions create an unstable surface and are only recommended for short periods of time. The goal is to relieve pressure on the perineal area.

Although the tips above are recommended specifically for the post-delivery phase, below are some general vulvar care guidelines that apply to you for your entire life. **This is information all women should know for a lifetime of good vulvar health. If you have a daughter, pass this information on to her. See Table 3.**

GUIDELINES FOR A LIFETIME OF GOOD VULVAR CARE

You should avoid using soap, cleansers or body wash on the vulvar region. The inner area of the vulva (known as the vestibule), or the vaginal opening (known as the introitus), can become irritated if you wash with regular soap. Part of the vestibule and the vagina and its opening are made of the same type of skin as the inside of your mouth. You would never consider washing your mouth with soap on a regular basis, and neither should you inside the vagina. If you use cleanser, do so externally only over the hair-bearing areas. Usually, an unscented cleanser (such as Cetaphil or Basis) is recommended.

Everyday products can irritate the vulva region. These products include deodorant soaps, bubble baths, shower gels, talcum powder, cleansing wipes, perfumed soaps and washes, deodorants, and antiseptics. This includes products that you use to wash your underwear. Such products may make your skin sore and uncomfortable. Also, watch out for skin irritants in personal care products, which can disrupt the tissue chemistry of the vagina (known as vaginal pH). If you are feeling particularly sensitive, avoid scented laundry soaps and dryer sheets, which contain irritating chemicals. You may want to wash your underwear separately and rinse it several times. Use menstrual pads that are deodorant free and made of cotton or natural fiber that does not irritate the skin.

Washing techniques can minimize discomfort in the vulva. The skin of the outer lips and inner lips (labia minora) should be washed only with water using the fingers on each side of the labia rather than a washcloth. You can also continue to use the peri bottle for specific cleansing, for example, after urination or a bowel movement. This helps minimize irritation from wiping with toilet paper. The peri bottle can also be used after sexual activity. Douching or squirting water up into the vagina is not necessary or recommended as the vagina cleans itself naturally. Over-washing can also cause problems and upset the natural balance of healthy vaginal bacteria. Both these techniques will minimize irritation of the sensitive vulvar skin.

Although shaving, waxing, and sugaring are common practices, hair growth in the vulvar area is natural and protective of the skin. Hair removal is not a practice that improves hygiene or is necessary in the post-partum period or beyond.

Good vulvar skin care means fresh air access to the region. Avoid wearing tight clothing that does not let the skin breathe. Wear underwear that has all cotton in the crotch portion or perineal area. This allows the skin to breathe and maximizes hygiene.

Table Three: Summary of Vulvar Care Guidelines

BEST VULVAR CARE AND PRACTICES	ACTIVITIES TO AVOID
Cotton material for undergarments and feminine hygiene products	Synthetic underwear, pantyhose and tights, non-cotton lining on menstrual pads
Loose fitting pants, skirts or athletic wear	Extended wearing of jeans or other tight pants, swimsuits, leotards, thongs or lycra garments
Washing clothing with unscented detergents and double rinsing	Washing with scented detergents
Specific vulvar cleansing with lukewarm or cool water only and use of fingertips. Pat dry, don't rub.	Washing or cleaning out the vagina, known as douching. Use of hot water, any soap or body wash and use of washcloths.
General bathing with fragrance-free pH neutral soap	Getting any soap or cleanser on the vulva. Using fragranced, harsh, or deodorant soaps that might contact the vulva during a shower or bath.
Alternating sitting activities with movement and standing. Use of ergonomic seats and cushions with prolonged sitting	Prolonged pressure on the perineum, uncomfortable or poorly fitting chairs or bicycle seats

TIP 2: YOUR PELVIC ROSTER—PERSONAL INVENTORY CHECK

"It just hurts, I'm not sure where"

The obstacles women encounter when they return to intercourse or sexual activity after childbirth are rarely discussed. After vaginal delivery, it is common for women to be concerned about resuming sexual activity. Some have already found that it is uncomfortable. Treatment for discomfort during sexual activity begins with understanding what is not working and what is hurting. It is important to be able to describe or show it to your partner or health care provider.

Sally's son was born six months ago. Sally has been unable to have intercourse because it feels like a knife is stabbing her when she attempts any vaginal penetration. She had an episiotomy and her doctor cleared her to have sex after her six-week post-partum visit. She tried that week, and she could not have intercourse. She returned to her doctor, who offered a numbing cream and a referral to see a physical therapist. Sally was surprised that there was physical therapy specifically for her condition.

One of the first steps for Sally was to help her identify where her symptoms were coming from. She wasn't familiar with her perineum or what hurt when she was touched.

Recovery starts when you can identify the problem. Observing and checking your body is a way to self-test if the area is pain free and ready for sexual activity, or to determine if you need some exercises before resuming activity.

This means you should look at your vulvar region with a mirror, move the skin, and map or identify the problem areas. Some women find this emancipating while others find it scary or disgusting. Regardless, it is important to understand your body and particularly your genitalia when you are trying to revive your sex life. This understanding can lead to discovery of problems and the return to a pleasurable sex life. Do what you are comfortable with, and engage your partner in the activity if you need support and help. Remember your goal and trust that knowledge of your body will help you resume sexually satisfying activity.

Just like any area of your body, the skin and muscles will need to heal before resuming full sexual activity. The general guideline is to wait six weeks after delivery before engaging in sex that involves vaginal penetration.

PREPARING FOR OBSERVATION

You'll need a handheld mirror and a comfortable position in order to observe the perineal area. I suggest that you also touch the areas of the perineum. This should be done with clean hands or you may wear a vinyl, nitrite exam glove if doing so makes you more comfortable.

There are three options for positioning. Choose the one that is most comfortable for you:

- Lie on your back with your head propped up on pillows. Drop your knees apart (put pillows beneath your knees to support them) and place your feet together.
- Sit on a toilet. Spread your legs apart so that you can see the perineum.
- Put one foot up on a bathtub ledge and place the mirror to see the perineum.

CHECKING YOUR PERINEUM

Checking your perineum includes looking with a mirror at your skin and vaginal opening, and testing your pelvic floor muscles. If you find problems, you can map and record the areas of pain and share this information with your doctor and partner. See Figure 4 for the anatomy of the region.

- With your mirror, identify the perineal body region. Look for skin irritation including redness, swelling, and scarring from stretching or episiotomy.
- Check for any tissues coming out of the vagina. Sometimes, if internal muscles and ligaments are stretched, the top wall of the vagina can drop down or prolapse. This is commonly called a cystocele, as it is the area of the vagina that shares support with the bladder. The back wall changes are called a rectocele and are associated with the area of the vagina that shares support with the rectum. Knowing these terms will help you communicate with your health care provider.

MOVING AND MAPPING YOUR PERINEUM

This technique is used to check the sensitivity of the perineal tissues and to see if they can move without pain. It is normal to feel some pull when the skin is stretched, or even a slight burn while the stretch is occurring, but you should not have pain after moving the skin, nor should there be tears (fissures) or bleeding as a result of moving the skin. Use the pain maps (figures 6 and 7) to identify and record the areas that are sensitive, and share your findings with your partner or doctor.

Figure 4 • The Perineum

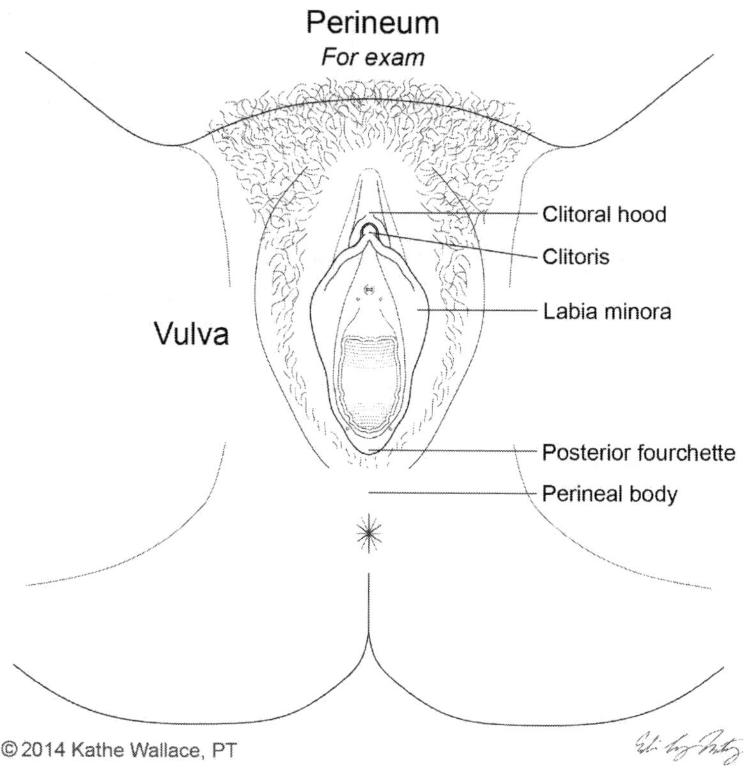

Now begin taking your own personal inventory by checking the specific areas listed below. Remember that each part is important to review. Don't worry if you think your parts don't specifically match pictures or how you think they "should" look; each person's parts will vary as much as each face in the world.

Labia

- Use your thumb and a finger to spread the vaginal lips (labia minora). Note if they can be moved without discomfort. Do this in two places: near the top of the opening and at the middle.

Clitoris and Clitoral Hood

- Use your thumb and a finger to lift the v-shaped hood to expose the clitoral glans. The glans is very sensitive as it has the most nerve endings of any organ and is specifically designed for pleasure. Note if it can be moved side to side and up and down without discomfort. The legs of the clitoris are underneath the labia majora and can't be felt directly.

Posterior Fourchette

- Continue to spread the lips (labia minora) and the vaginal opening but focus on the bottom part of the vagina. Note if it can be moved without discomfort.

Perineal Body/ Episiotomy Scar

- Touch and move the skin between the vaginal opening and the anus as demonstrated in Figure 5. Move the skin side to side, up and down, and at an angle. If this area is tender or painful, try the activities in Tips 6 and 7.

Figure 5 • Hand Placement for Perineal Body and Episiotomy Scar Examination

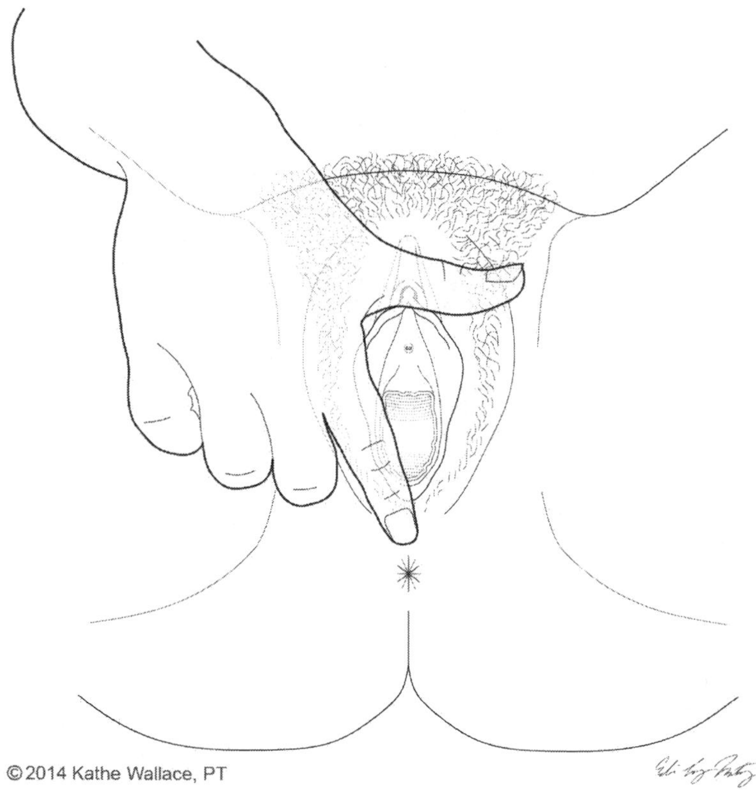

Recording the problem areas

The numbers represent a clock face with 12 being the area closest to the pubic bone and 6 the area closest to the anus. The 3 o'clock position will be on your left, 9 o'clock on your right. Once you find a problem area, record it with an X on Figure 6. Share the location of the discomfort with your partner. Usually these are the areas that could make sexual activity hurt with initial penetration or at the entrance.

Figure 6 • Recording Circle for Symptoms

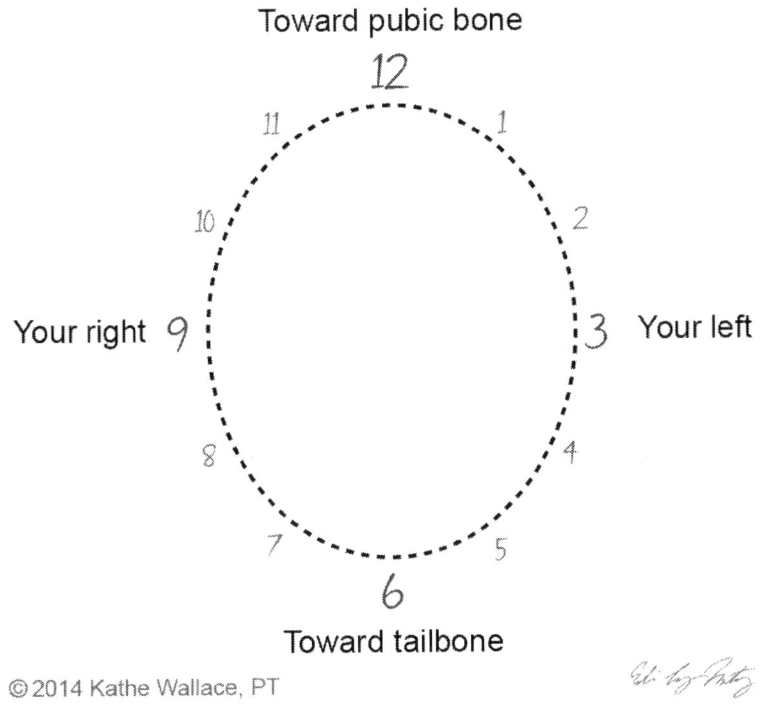

Vagina check

If your pain or symptoms are located inside the vagina, use a lubricated finger to touch the walls inside the vagina. The vaginal canal is a tube in which you should be able to feel the walls and assess if there is a problem at a specific depth versus the complete tube. Identify the location and side that creates symptoms and record on the diagram in Figure 7.

When touching inside the vagina, be aware that the walls have texture and are typically not smooth. The touch should not cause you discomfort.

Note any areas of discomfort as you perform the inside check at three different layers and the tissue inside the vagina.

1. Place your lubricated finger at the vaginal opening and insert it to your first knuckle sweeping it side to side around the canal and feeling at the level of the first layer of muscle.
2. Insert your finger further to the second knuckle and sweep to check the second layer of muscle.
3. Insert to the level of the third knuckle and sweep to complete the inside check at the third layer of muscle.

Figure 7 • Mapping the Vaginal Canal

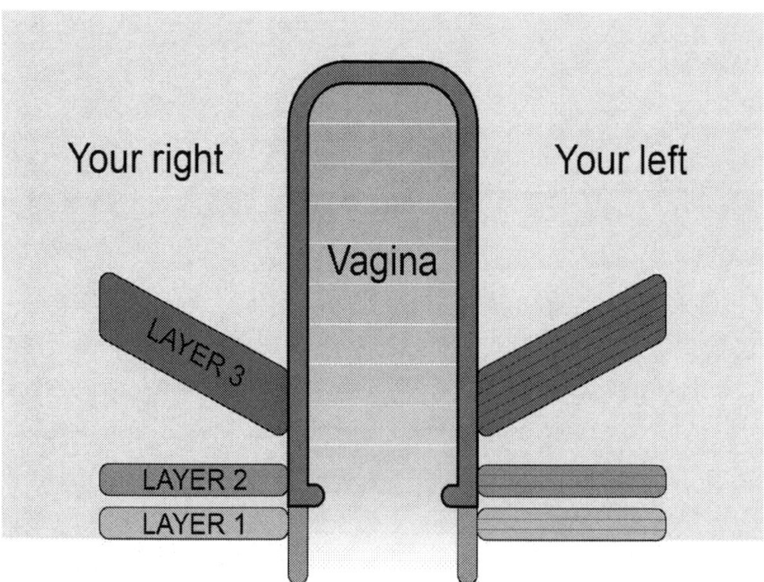

CONTRACTING THE PELVIC FLOOR

Next, try a pelvic floor contraction (Kegel exercise) and release while you are looking with a mirror. (See Tips 4, 5, and 8 for pelvic floor exercises.) A pelvic floor contraction will tighten the vaginal and anal openings. Release after a few seconds and notice if the vagina and the anus can let go or if it is hard to let them relax. Tightening and releasing should not be painful. Note if you experience any pain.

In summary, carefully mapping and gently contracting the pelvic floor can give you a lot of information about where your pain is coming from and how to move forward with treatment.

Sally was able to identify that her episiotomy site was most painful on the right side at the opening around 9 o'clock. She also found that all the layers of muscle bothered her more on the right than the left. She could share that with her husband and begin some specific stretching to the skin and muscles on that side. When she began to have intercourse, I encouraged her to be in sexual intercourse positions where she was on top and could direct and control the penetration depth and direction. She "steered to the left" and had pain-free intercourse for the first time after delivery without using a numbing cream. The numbing cream works only on the skin, and Sally needed work on her muscles.

If you have pain at any of the external sites, you will need to do some work with the episiotomy or tear site. (See Tip 6.) If you experience pain with a contraction or deeper in the vagina, you will benefit from internal stretching exercises. (See Tip 7.)

If you notice few specific pains at the opening but feel generally stretched out and weak, strengthening and engaged breathing will help you (see Tip 8).

TIP 3: DRY AND PAINFUL PARTS—VAGINAL LUBRICATION AFTER CHILDBIRTH

"I feel like my vagina is a desert full of sandpaper sensations."

Normally, lubrication of the vagina occurs when there is sexual desire and arousal. However, sometimes foreplay and desire are not enough for a post-partum woman. Vaginal dryness is very common during the post-partum period especially if you are breastfeeding. This dryness can cause friction and discomfort during sexual activity. Finding the right lubricant can be an easy fix to avoiding sandpaper-like sex. Be proactive and try a variety of lubricants to help you achieve pain-free sexual activity.

It is rather common to think the lack of lubrication is just due to aging, but in fact, childbirth, nursing, and normal hormone changes with your menstrual cycle can also cause changes in the ability of the vagina to lubricate naturally with arousal. The lack of lubrication does not mean that there is no sexual desire. Be aware that medications that work for anxiety and depression can alter your desire and lubrication. Also, avoid soap on the vulva and watch out for skin irritants in personal care products, which can disrupt the tissue chemistry of the vagina (known as vaginal pH).

Lubrication works to help ease entry into the vagina by coating the opening and internal tissues. Apply the lubricant with your fingers to your labia and around the vaginal opening. Also apply it to your partner's finger or penis, or to a vibrator or dildo. Sometimes I suggest using an applicator to place the lubricant inside the vagina as well as on the outside. The amount to use varies with the type of lubricant you have chosen, usually a few drops of silicone- based to between a teaspoon and a tablespoon of water-based. Ultimately, the product that feels best and works for you is the one to use. Sometimes it takes a few trials to find the right one.

Lubricants come in several different bases and many ingredients that are designed to easily produce a slip-and-slide sensation with sexual activity.

- **Water-based products** work well with condoms as well as sex toys and easily rinse off. They are usually odorless and colorless. You may need to reapply this lubricant during sex as they tend to easily absorb into the skin. Common recommended brands are Slippery Stuff and Good Clean Love because they are free of ingredients that can cause irritation.
- **Oil-based products** provide a thick coating and a lot of staying power. Some ob/gyn doctors recommend using coconut oil. Oil-based products, whether they are from a plant, animal, or petroleum source, can weaken latex condoms. Therefore, they are not recommended if you are using condoms for birth control or sexually transmitted disease prevention. They also can degrade some sex toys made of latex.
- **Silicone-based lubricants** provide lasting lubrication but are slick and sometimes harder to rinse off. They do work in water and don't dry out making them versatile and known for their endurance. Silicone products are recommended by many gynecologists and sexologists for their patients who have sensitive skin. If you are using sex toys, be sure the manufacturer certifies its silicone toys are compatible with silicone lubricants. A common recommended brand is Pjur Woman Bodyglide.

- **Hybrids** have a combination or ratio of oil, silicone, and/or water as a final product. A common recommended brand is Sliquid Silk.

READ THE LABELS!

A lot of times you'll read a list of ingredients that it seems only a chemistry teacher can pronounce. Here are several of the most common ingredients that make water-based lubricants slippery but can cause potential problems for women. Ultimately, several products could meet your needs, but some of the ingredients may be irritating to your skin and sensitive vulvar area.

- **Glycerin** – A sugar-based product that can lead to yeast infections. It can also be quite sticky.
- **Parabens** – A common preservative. There is debate on the health risk of parabens because of estrogenic (meaning it slightly mimics estrogen) activity. Because there is usually only a small amount of parabens in personal-care products, some people do not consider the amount harmful. Parabens may be listed on the product label as methylparaben, popylparaben, ethylparaben, butylparaben, or benzylparaben.
- **Propylene glycol** – A colorless liquid derived from natural gas. It is an additive in many foods, toiletries, household, and automobile products, usually used to keep things from drying out. It is an ingredient in many water-based lubricants to control the thickness of the product and sometimes the fragrance. Many people with sensitive or irritated skin do not do well with this additive.

If the product has something added for taste, temperature, or scent, the likelihood of irritation to the skin is greater. These products are usually not recommended when you have persistent post-partum pain. If your vulva is sensitive, these options should be avoided. You might want to consider organic water-based lubricant products.

Ultimately, the product that feels best and works for you is the one to use. There is a lot to know on lubricants for sexual activity and sometimes it takes a few trials to find the right one.

TIP 4: LETTING GO — RELAX-AND-RELEASE BREATHING

Pain and discomfort in the vaginal region is common after childbirth. You may be experiencing muscle tension due to vaginal pain and be caught in a cycle of keeping the muscles in the pelvic and genital regions tight. A practiced and purposeful relaxation-breathing pattern helps to release and reduce tension. It also clears your mind to experience the sensations of your body. If you are experiencing pain and/or anxiety with attempts of vaginal penetration or vulvar vaginal touch, this technique is for you. It focuses on using the most efficient breathing muscle of the body: the diaphragm. Using diaphragmatic breathing is calming to the nervous system. It is also an important step prior to engaging in sexual activity or any activities that stretch or move restricted muscles.

The diaphragm is a dome-shaped muscle located at the base of your ribs. On the inhalation, your diaphragm moves downward into the belly, which makes your abdomen rise. The rise of your abdomen causes your ribs to move sideways, like an umbrella opening. Letting your belly move and your ribs expand is the natural and most efficient way to breathe. If you watch your baby breathe while he or she sleeps, you will see that babies naturally breathe into their bellies. As adults we often need to relearn this type of breathing. This type of breathing does not need to be forced, but it does require practice to do effectively.

In order to get the most benefit from relax-and-release breathing, lie comfortably on your back with your legs in a relaxed position (bent or straight) and your hands resting on your belly. Also pay attention to the pelvic floor muscles. To encourage relaxation, allow the pelvic floor to move outward with the breath.

- When you breathe in, allow your belly to rise up and out and think of your pelvic muscles as softening and moving toward your feet. (See Figure 8.) As you practice relax-and-release breathing, hold a mental picture of the pelvic muscles descending and the sitting bones widening or flaring to make more space for the muscles. This relaxes the pelvic floor.
- Repeat this 3 times per day for 1–5 minutes each session.

Figure 8 • Pelvic Floor Release Breathing

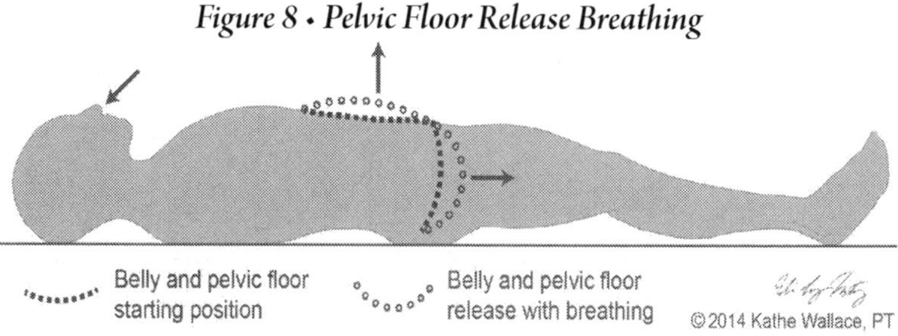

HELPFUL HINTS FOR RELAX-AND-RELEASE BREATHING

- Place your tongue at the top of your mouth with your teeth slightly apart. This allows your jaw to relax and allows you to take a relaxed breath.
- Breathe in (inhale) through your nose and let your nostrils flare.
- Allow your ribs to expand to the sides and back while your belly rises.
- Pause for a few seconds at the top of the in-breath.
- Blow out (exhale) the air slowly through your mouth by slightly puckering the lips. The lip position creates a slight resistance and allows the air to flow out gradually.
- Spend a longer time on the out-breath than the in-breath. Count to 4 as you inhale, pause, and then slowly exhale to the count of 8.
- Try the breathing with different leg positioning; for your comfort you may want to place a pillow under your knees.
- If you are doing this as preparation for sexual activity, try this breathing with a different leg position. Bend your hips and knees slightly and place the soles of your feet together, allowing your knees to fall open to each side. If there is too much pull on your inner thigh, support your knees with pillows.

TIP 5: IF IT HURTS BEFORE YOU START— EXERCISES TO RELEASE THE PELVIC FLOOR

By learning to release the pelvic floor muscles, you can potentially feel less pain or pressure in your pelvis, bladder, and genital regions at rest and with sexual activity. If you have pain with vaginal penetration, practice this technique first, before sexual activity. It can also be used during sexual foreplay as a "warm up" to vaginal penetration in order to release and enjoy sexual activity.

The pelvic floor is a group of muscles that support the bottom part of your pelvis from the pubic bone to the tailbone. The muscles surrounding the vagina, urethra, and rectum can affect bladder, bowel, or sexual function. If the muscles—commonly called the pelvic floor or Kegel muscles—are too tight, they can cause pain with penetration. There are exercises typically prescribed when a woman needs pelvic floor strengthening. The release exercise is sometimes called the Reverse Kegel as it focuses on the "letting go," or relaxing, part of the muscle movement. Some post-partum women have excessive tension in the pelvic floor muscles around the vagina, which creates tenderness with attempts at vaginal penetration. It is important to know where all the muscle layers are located.

FINDING AND RELEASING THE PELVIC FLOOR MUSCLES

The pelvic floor muscles have surface and deep layers, and you need to find and release all of them. Surface muscles surround the bladder, vagina, and anal openings. Deep muscles support the bladder, rectum, and vagina. The muscles attach to the pelvic bones. For maximum release, it is helpful to imagine you are widening your sitting bones and moving the tailbone away from the pubic bone.

PERFORMING THE PELVIC FLOOR RELEASING ACTIVITY

It is a good idea to practice pelvic floor releasing with or without the breathing techniques mentioned above on a daily basis. Start with 1–5 minutes at least twice per day to learn what release feels like in your pelvic region.

Also consider doing these exercises prior to sexual activity—perhaps as foreplay!

Figure 9 • Surface/External Muscles Opening: Widening the Sitting Bones

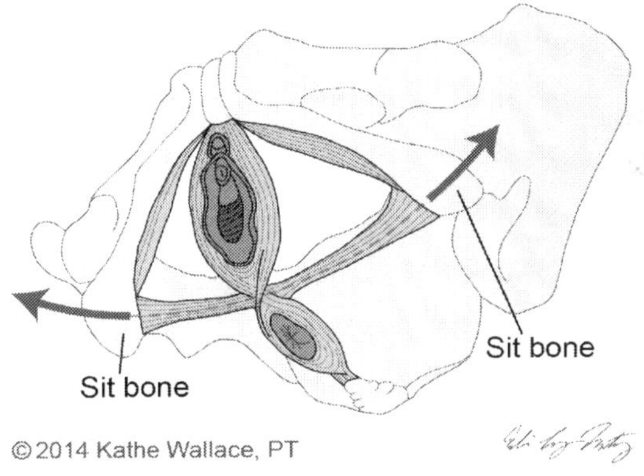

Figure 10 • Deep/Internal Muscles Dropping: Moving the Tailbone away from the Pubic Bone

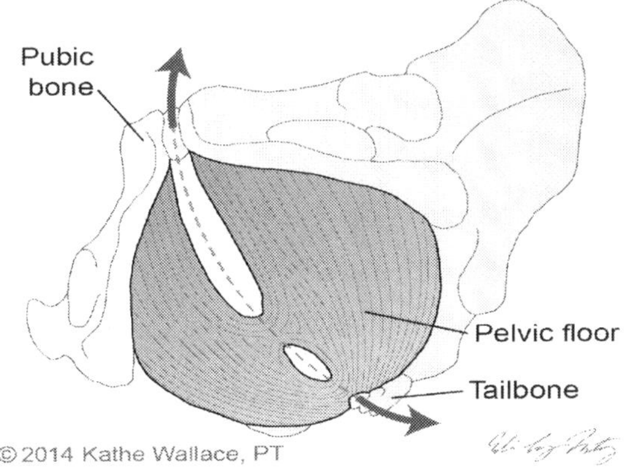

HELPFUL HINTS TO RELEASE PELVIC FLOOR MUSCLES

- Use a mirror to look at the perineal body and anus area. Think of the muscles as dropping and opening by imagining the release of a bowel movement or the start of urination. Sometimes gently bulging the belly outward, making it into a beach ball shape, helps to release and drop the muscles.
- When doing the exercise above, consider using the imagery of a circle opening wider. You could also try thinking about a rose blossoming or the tailbone moving or "wagging" like a happy puppy.
- Without you knowing it, the pelvic floor muscles can tighten with stress and worry. Therefore, take time to reduce stress and worry.
- Sometimes the simple awareness of muscle tightness can help you relax and release. Check in with your body frequently to see if you are holding the pelvic floor muscles too tightly.
- Sitting on the toilet is a natural time to release your pelvic floor muscles. Pay attention to the feelings in your pelvic floor and pelvis when you are emptying your bladder or bowels. Eventually, practice releasing your pelvic floor muscles while sitting on a chair instead of the toilet.

If you still are experiencing difficulty, see a physical therapist. One of the things he or she can do is use biofeedback to help you "get to know" the tension in your pelvic floor and teach you more ways to release it.

If you are experiencing bladder symptoms of urinary urgency and frequency and have been evaluated and told you do not have a bladder infection, it is possible that the pelvic floor muscles may be too tense and be contributing to your symptoms. This pelvic floor release technique could help relieve your symptoms.

TIP 6: WHAT TO DO IF YOU TORE DURING DELIVERY—WORKING WITH AN EPISIOTOMY OR PERINEAL TEARS

If you had an episiotomy or a tear as a result of childbirth, you have a scar. Even though not all tears after childbirth require stitches for repair, there is usually a certain amount of tissue stretching and/or tearing that can create scarring. This scarring can be painful and restrict the skin mobility if not moved. Moving the scar, through mobilization and massage, is a good idea prior to attempting sexual activity. It is common practice to massage scars after orthopedic surgeries for your knee or shoulder, but rarely is a new mom taught techniques for massaging an episiotomy scar or a childbirth tear. Here are some basic techniques that will help you achieve normal mobility and prepare you for pain-free sexual activity. These techniques can be done on your own or with the help of a partner.

You can begin to lightly massage your scar once the incision has healed, usually six weeks after delivery. But even if it has been longer than six weeks after delivery, it is not too late to begin massage. Starting scar massage even two years after its creation can be beneficial. Some women see results in just a few sessions of massaging, though women with third- and fourth-degree tears (see Table 1) may take six weeks or longer to see results. It is important to know that a scar will appear pink or red and slightly raised for the first few weeks but will flatten over time into a white line.

HOW TO MOBILIZE AND MASSAGE

To begin, make sure your hands are clean. Set aside 15 minutes for the techniques. Get in a comfortable reclined position, legs apart. Some women use the empty tub after a bath, as they are well supported and relaxed. If you have trouble doing any of these scar motions and massage, you may need a small amount of lubricant on your fingers. When the skin is stretched using mild to moderate pressure, expect to feel a light burning or pull. You should not feel sharp pain or have persistent pain more than a few minutes after the massage. Use a scale of 0–10, with 10 being the most intense pain possible. To avoid persistent discomfort keep the intensity below a 5.

The massage should be done one time per day or every other day. To maximize your comfort begin by moving the scar and skin in the directions that causes the least discomfort, holding a gentle stretch 5-15 seconds. Do the movements between 5-10 times. If you identify a specific area and direction that moves the least (from tip 2), gradually massage it to mobilize the area. When the area of discomfort is both inside and outside of the vagina you can also perform the sweep and scar rolling techniques. If you are having difficulty with these techniques, ask your health care provider for a referral to a pelvic floor physical therapist.

MASSAGE TECHNIQUES

Place your finger pad on the scar near the vaginal opening. Move the scar slowly by first moving it side-to-side. Then move the scar up- and- down. See figures 11 and 12.

Figure 11 • Side-to-Side Stretch

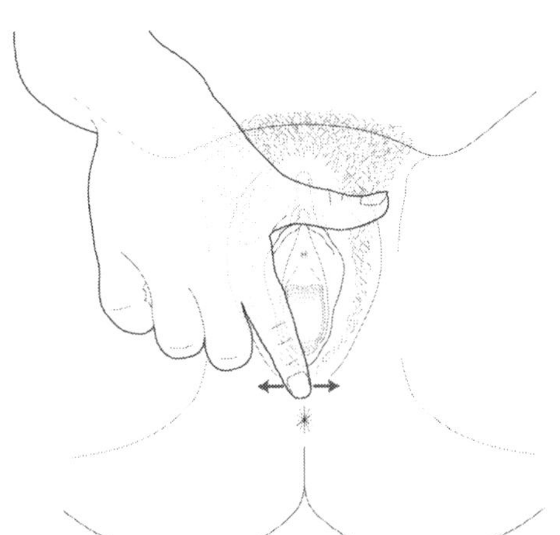

Figure 12 • Up-and-Down Stretch

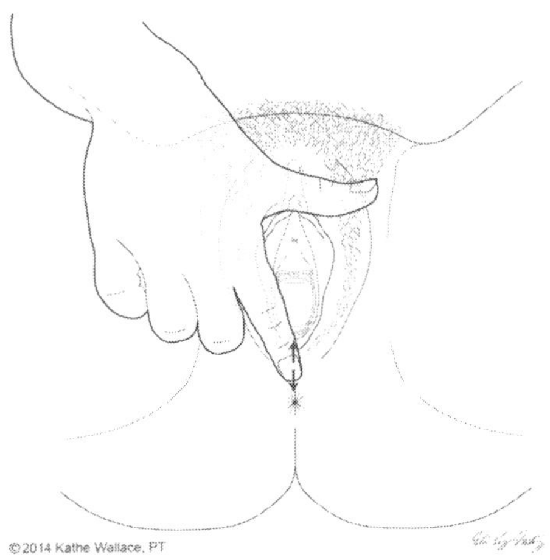

SCAR ROLLING

Place your thumb on the inside of your vagina and your forefinger (the pointer finger) on the outside. Roll the scar between your thumb and your forefinger. See figure 13.

Figure 13 • Scar Rolling

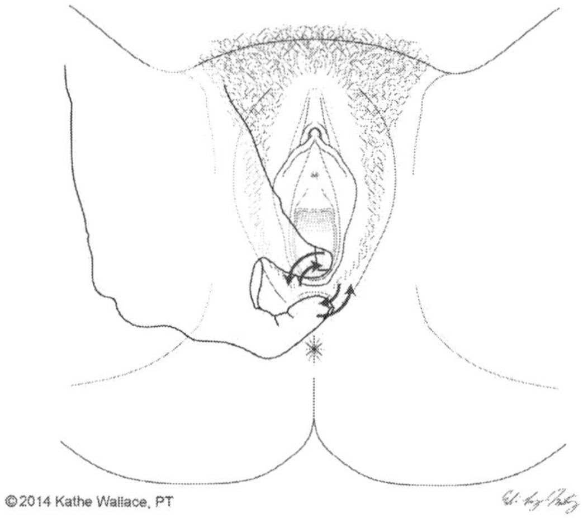

©2014 Kathe Wallace, PT

OTHER STRETCHES

You can also move out from the center like you are drawing a star on your perineal body area. Finally move the scar in circular clockwise and counter-clockwise directions to maximize the mobility in all directions.

Figure 14 • Sweeping

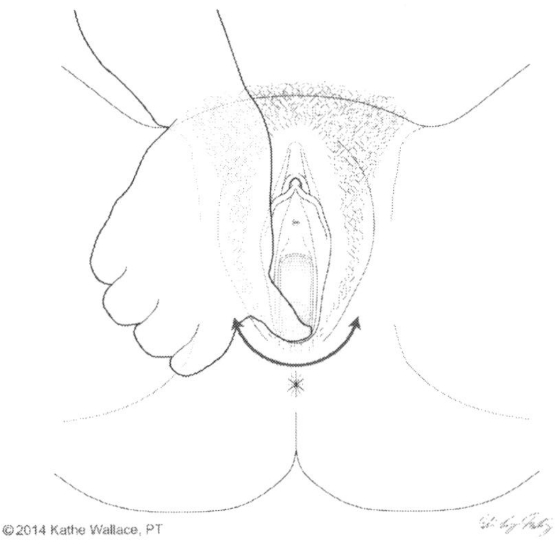

SWEEPING

Place your thumb at the lower half of the vaginal opening. Use the thumb pad to sweep inside the vaginal opening between 3 o'clock and 9 o'clock (if you think of the opening like a clock face with 6 o'clock toward the anus), use gentle pressure and sweep from side to side. Imagine you are drawing a half circle image with your thumb. See figure 14.

You can also try this in different positions. Sometimes it is easier to perform the skin and scar stretch after a shower or while sitting on a toilet. Put one foot up on a bathtub ledge or toilet seat and try the same techniques. Alternatively you can do the sweep technique on a toilet. Check in with your muscles and make sure you are not tensing the pelvic floor muscles during these alternate position techniques.

TIP 7: WHEN IT HURTS WITH PENETRATION— INTERNAL STRETCHING OF THE VAGINA AND PELVIC FLOOR MUSCLES, INCLUDING TRIGGER POINT AND SCAR TISSUE RELEASE

Attempting to return to sexual activity with tight pelvic floor muscles or restricted scars can be painful. In the post-partum period, you are likely to be sore at the perineum or inside the vagina. Just like any area of your body, the soreness can cause muscle guarding and tension. Sometimes vaginal delivery results in pelvic floor trigger points—sensitive, painful areas in your muscles. If you had a tear or episiotomy that extended to or through the back wall of the vagina, you could also have persistent discomfort with penetration if that scar is not mobilized. As odd as it seems, the pulling and stretching from a vaginal delivery can create a need to stretch tight muscles in the pelvic floor. The following techniques are for the muscles, fascia, and scar tissue. They are commonly called myofascial techniques and are used to prevent or alleviate any pain or discomfort with vaginal penetration or contact after childbirth. This tip will teach you techniques to stretch the vaginal muscles that attach to the pelvis and release trigger points in the muscles that create painful symptoms.

A general guideline is to wait six weeks after giving birth before resuming intercourse or any type of vaginal penetration. These techniques describe stretching tissues that are inside the vagina, so you should also wait until your six-week mark to try these. You should be comfortable with stretching the outer skin and surface muscles before you try internal vaginal stretching or trigger point release. (See Tip 6.) The ultimate goal with stretching the vaginal walls and pelvic floor muscles is to have flexibility in all directions so that daily activities and intercourse are more comfortable.

The pelvic floor muscles are harder to stretch than most muscles. Pelvic floor muscles attach to the pelvic girdle bones. These bones form a ring and don't have movable joints like your knee or elbow. It really is not possible for most women to completely stretch or release the pelvic floor muscles without some internal stretching. The stretching techniques described below are designed specifically for this difficult-to-stretch pelvic floor and perineal area of the body.

Pelvic floor trigger points can be the cause of pain with intercourse. Trigger points can feel like tight bands of muscle or a specific point or muscle knot that when touched cause your pain or symptoms. These points can be accessed with your finger, a wand, or dilator, depending on the location within the pelvic floor. The trigger points or taut muscles are treated by pressing on the point with moderate pressure and holding that for up to a minute and a half. Pressing harder on a trigger point will not get the muscle to release. It is sometimes helpful to stroke the muscle along the tight band, or strum across it.

WHAT TO USE FOR INTERNAL STRETCHING TECHNIQUES

These techniques can be done with a finger, dilator, or wand. Some women will start with their own fingers (gloved or washed prior to insertion) to see if they can feel and stretch any painful spots or restrictions internally. If the painful spot is beyond the reach of a finger, a tool becomes necessary.

There are many things that can be used as stretching tools. A tampon with a firm plastic applicator or an empty applicator for vaginal medications might be a good item to use for the first insertion. You could also use a vaginal-sized vibrator. Several types of tools are available see KatheWallace.com/bookresources. These include sets of vaginal dilators or individual wands. Vaginal dilators consist of a set of cylinders that come in progressive sizes so you can gently stretch the muscles and the vaginal opening. They can be purchased with or without handles which can assist in placement and stretching. A pelvic floor massage wand comes in different sizes. It is curved with a tapered end so that you can reach trigger points and stretch the pelvic floor muscles. If you start with a dilator or wand use a small size so you are able to place it comfortably. Think of all these tools as an extension of your finger.

MONITOR YOUR STRETCH AND RELEASE INTENSITY

Trigger point and scar tissue release can be uncomfortable but should not be painful. When performing the techniques, you should use a personal pain/pressure scale to monitor the intensity of the myofascial and trigger point treatment. On a 0–10 scale, with 10 being the most intense, start with tolerable or comfortable pressure of 2–3 or less.

As you increase the pressure, stay in a range of 3–6 on your pressure/pain scale. Hold the pressure on the trigger point or painful location within the muscle beginning with 15–30 seconds and working up to 90 seconds.

POSITIONING

Comfort and relaxation are key to stretching the pelvic floor muscles. Choose a position that supports your head and shoulders so that you can reach the vaginal area with ease. Many women choose an empty warm bathtub because it offers back and leg support and is located in a private room in the home. Alternatively you can lie on your back with pillows under your head and shoulders. Place your hips in a flexed position with your knees supported and apart.

BEGINNING INSTRUCTIONS AND TECHNIQUES

Set aside at least 15 minutes for these exercises so that you have ample time for the process.

- **Start with relaxation techniques.** Do a few relaxed breaths. Try a contraction (close and lift) of the pelvic floor muscles followed by a release. If a contraction is painful, try pelvic floor releasing exercises (see Tip 5) before you begin the stretching.
- **Check your muscle tension.** The goal is to be aware of muscles that are not relaxed before you start the stretching and to increase your awareness of any muscle tension that is present. This tension check and awareness can greatly reduce pain with penetration. (See Tip 5 for help with this.)
- **Apply lubricant.** Start with a tablespoon or more. Spread open the vaginal lips (labia) so that you can apply a moderate amount of lubricant near the opening. Apply additional lubricant to the end of the dilator, wand, applicator or inserting finger. If insertions are difficult due to internal dryness you can place lubricant into an applicator (3cc size) and apply it internally. The amount and placement of lubricant will vary from person to person and product to product. Be sure you apply a lubricant product that works for you. (See Tip 3.)

- **Initial placement.** Hold the labia minora (vaginal lips) apart and place the finger or tip of the tool at the opening of the vagina. Angle the finger or tool end slightly downward toward your tailbone as you place it in the vagina. This avoids hitting the more sensitive structures of the urethra at the top of the opening. Check again that your muscles are relaxed. Slowly insert a finger or a tool stopping at the area when you feel resistance or pain. You are now ready for specific techniques.

IMPORTANT TECHNIQUE AND SAFETY TIPS FOR PERFORMING INTERNAL VAGINAL STRETCHING WITH A FINGER, WAND, OR DILATOR

1. To help the muscles respond to stretch or trigger point release, you may find it helpful to take a warm bath or apply warm compresses or a heating pad for 10 minutes externally over the perineum.

2. The key to trigger point and stretching treatment is to lengthen the muscles. The goal is to stretch the muscles within the pelvis. You should not feel tingling, numbness, or pulsing. Those sensations are associated with nerves and blood vessels and should be avoided.

3. Change the direction of pressure rather than the intensity of the pressure. More pressure is not better. Do not let the sensations be too intense or exceed a pain level of 6 on a 0–10 scale. Avoid forcing or pushing too hard with your finger or a tool.

4. Do not direct the stretches upward toward the pubic bone between 10 and 2 o'clock. This is where the bladder and urethra are located. If you believe you need stretching in this area talk to your health care provider.

5. Start stretching gradually beginning with 5 - 15 seconds. Limit each stretch or trigger point release to a 60–90 second maximum with an equal rest period between. Also limit the total time to 10–15 minutes, one time per day.

6. After internal stretching techniques, some people find application or reapplication of heat helpful, or you may find cold more soothing. Limit application time of heat or cold to 10 minutes maximum.

7. Follow the tool cleaning and storage care instructions from the manufacturer.

SPECIFIC PELVIC FLOOR STRETCHES

There are several types of internal stretches described below. The techniques can be done with a finger, dilator, or wand. They are designed to help you gradually stretch and mobilize the vaginal tissues and the pelvic floor muscles. Follow the safety tips and beginning placement instructions for proper positioning and lubrication.

Hold each stretch initially for 5 seconds and build up tolerance to 15–60 seconds. Take 2–3 relaxing deep breaths between stretches. Repeat the stretches 3–5 times in a row once a day. Use these techniques every other day unless instructed by your health care provider to do otherwise.

Remember that stretching can be accomplished with a finger or a tool. These figures depict the techniques being accomplished with a tool.

DOWNWARD STRETCH

Place a finger or a dilator at the vaginal opening, insert it into the vagina 1–3 inches or as far as is comfortable. Check that your muscles are relaxed. Then gently press toward the tailbone (toward the 6 o'clock position). See figure 15.

Figure 15 • Downward Stretch with a Dilator

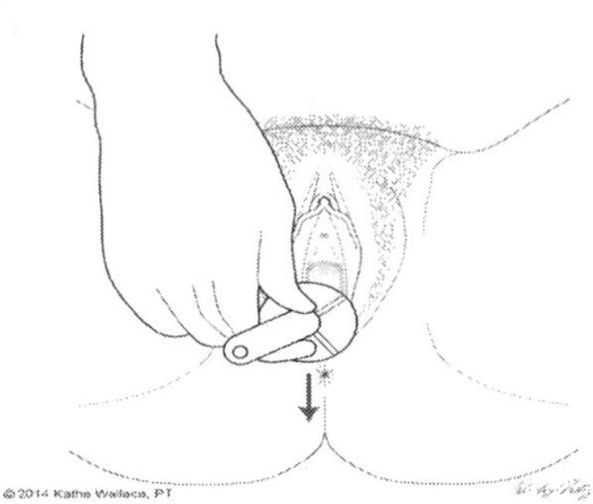

SIDE WALL STRETCH

Once in position stretch the muscles by gently pushing to the side walls of the vagina. The side of the vaginal wall is being stretched with the length of the finger or dilator. If you think about the vagina as a clock, the stretching occurs at either the 3 o'clock and 9 o'clock positions (see figure 16). This will stretch all layers of one side of the vagina. This side wall stretch can also be done at the 4 o'clock and 8 o'clock positions.

Figure 16 • Side Wall Stretch with a Dilator

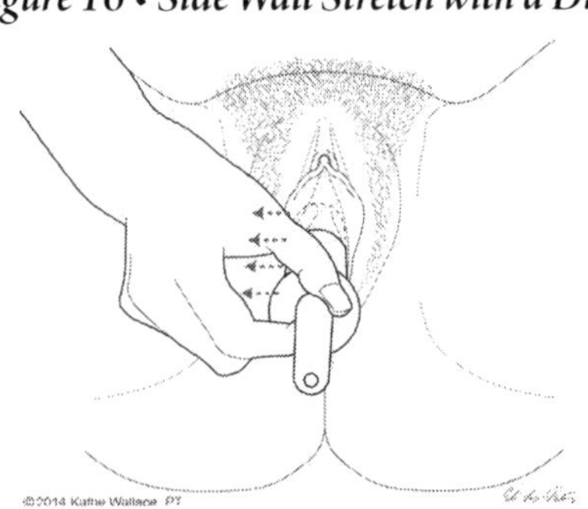

ANGLED STRETCH

Use the finger or dilator to stretch the deeper muscles by angling the tip toward the back and sidewalls (see figure 17). You can also aim specifically for a trigger point or a place in your vagina that feels tender.

Figure 17 • Angled Stretch with a Dilator

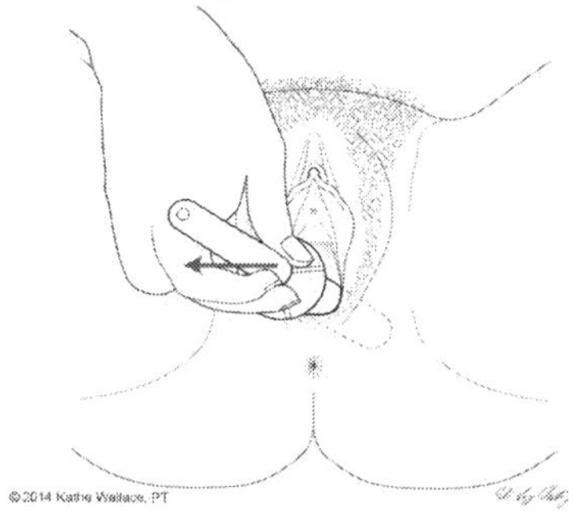

©2014 Kathe Wallace, PT

OTHER STRETCHES

Slowly practice moving the dilator in and out of the vagina. Also try moving the dilator in circles at the opening and along the vaginal walls to stretch the skin and muscles.

SPECIFIC MASSAGE TOOL OR WAND TECHNIQUES

There are two types of internal stretches described below that use the curved wand. They are designed to help you massage and/or release pelvic floor muscle trigger points.

Hold initially for 15 seconds and build up your tolerance to 60–90 seconds. Take 2–3 relaxing deep breaths between stretches when you release pressure from the wand. Repeat the stretching sweeps 3–5 times. The goal is to feel the discomfort ease and release with each repetition.

TRIGGER POINT TECHNIQUE

Trigger point pressure treatment is performed with a continuous hold of pressure on the muscle knot or tight area. See figure 18. This technique can also be performed with a dilator.

Figure 18 • Wand on Internal Trigger Point

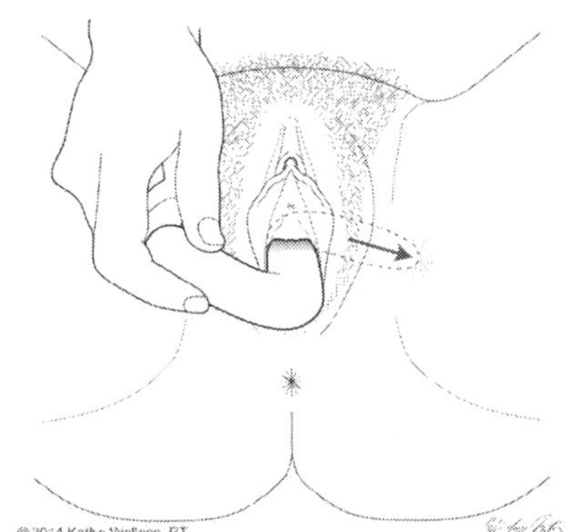

PELVIC FLOOR SWEEP MASSAGE

Slowly practice sweeping the wand across the muscles with gentle to moderate pressure. There is a specific sweep range identified in figure 20. Work one side of the opening from 2 o'clock to 6 o'clock on your left and from 10 o'clock to 6 o'clock position on your right.

Figure 19 • Wand Sweep

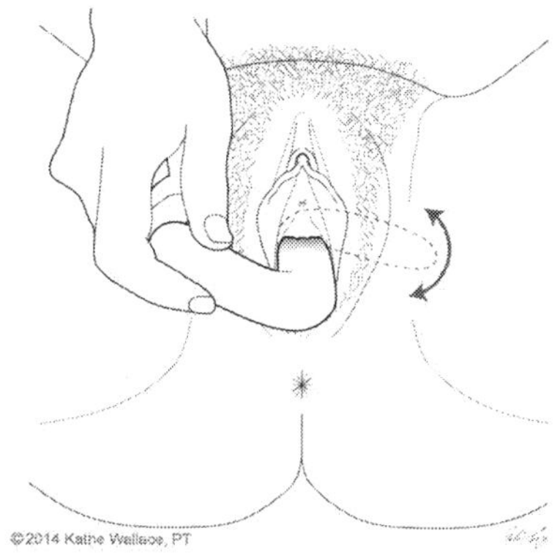

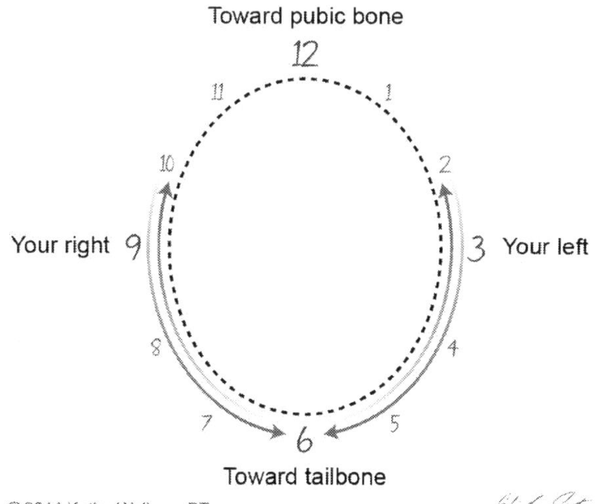

TIP 8: FEELING LOOSE OR DIFFERENT IN THE VAGINA—EXERCISES FOR STRENGTHENING PELVIC FLOOR MUSCLES

During vaginal birth, pelvic floor muscles are sometimes torn and always overstretched. This can cause weakness of the muscles. It can be a challenge for the post-partum mother to return these muscles to optimum function without a specific, dedicated exercise program. Returning to sexual activity involves understanding that weak muscles can cause changes in vaginal sensation after delivery and change the experience of intercourse and vaginal penetration. However, these techniques will help enhance sensation to revive enjoyable sexual activities. In addition to improving sexual function, strengthening the pelvic floor muscles also helps control urine leakage and diminishes the feeling of the organs falling out of the vagina.

Strong pelvic floor muscles improve sexual function. When the pelvic floor muscles contract, they close the vaginal walls. This tightening and closing enhances sexual sensation during vaginal penetration both for the woman and her male partner. Some of the muscles attach to the clitoris, move it, and assist in clitoral erection. Some women report an aroused sexual state when using these muscles during sexual activity, or simply while doing pelvic floor strengthening exercises. When all the muscles are stronger, they contribute to orgasm intensity and appreciation.

Locate the pelvic floor muscles. The pelvic floor muscles support the bottom part of the pelvis. They form a sling from the pubic bone to the tailbone that surrounds and supports the urethra, vagina, and rectum. (See Figures 21a and 21b)

Learn to use the pelvic floor muscles with imagery. The pelvic floor muscles have three layers. For simplicity, the first two layers will be called the external or surface portion (because you can see the effects of the muscles contracting). The external portion is responsible for ***opening and closing*** the bladder, vaginal, and rectal openings. When using the external portion of the muscles, it's helpful to imagine an elevator door opening and closing. The deep or internal portion (the third layer) is responsible for lifting and lowering the muscles. When using the internal portion of the pelvic floor muscles, it's helpful to think of elevator cables **moving *up and down.***

Figure 21a • Surface/External Muscles

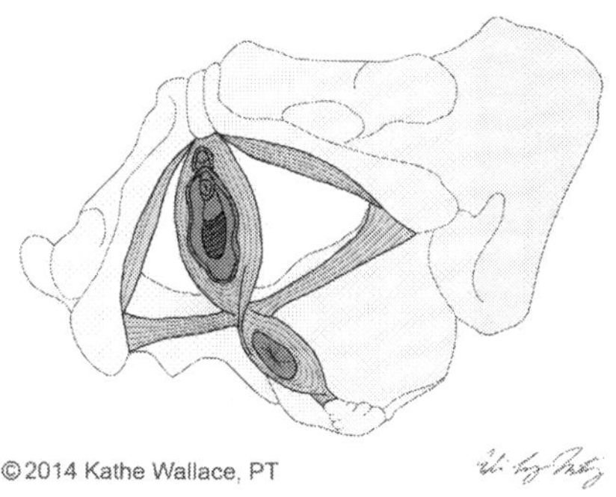

Figure 21b• Deep/Internal Muscles

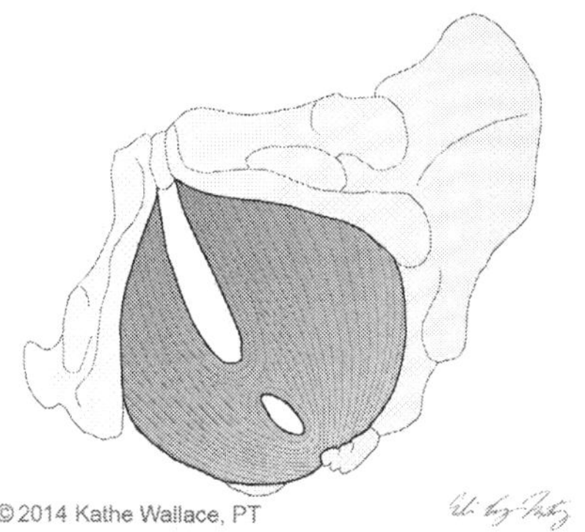

PELVIC FLOOR CONTRACTIONS ARE COMMONLY KNOWN AS KEGEL EXERCISES.

Steps for Pelvic Floor Muscle Contractions

- Close the openings of the surface pelvic floor muscles. Tighten the vaginal and rectal openings and visualize moving the clitoris (nodding it) while you squeeze and ***close*** the vaginal and bladder openings (like an elevator door).
- Lift the deep internal muscles up and in. As you lift, remember the span of the muscle sling that creates the floor and both the rectal and vaginal openings. Imagine you are lifting the entire sling from the back to the front (like the elevator ascending upward).

A complete exercise program of the pelvic floor includes activating and training all of the muscles in specific ways. Since sexual activity could be considered an athletic event, let's use a basic exercise training principle known as FITT, which stands for **Frequency**, **Intensity**, **Time,** and **Type** of exercise.

Frequency: If you feel your muscles are weak, it is better to do fewer but more frequent sets of exercises each day. For example, try 4 repetitions 6 times per day, contracting for a total of 24 times per day. When you are stronger, do more at a time in sets of 10. Quality is better than quantity. The ultimate goal is to do 3 sets of 10 endurance and quick contractions per day, as described below.

Intensity: The intensity does not need to be a maximum effort contraction; research shows that muscles gain strength and endurance when worked at 60–80% of maximum effort. Don't work too hard, but make the muscle do more than it is used to.

Time: The time of the contractions for a quick pulse contraction is a brief second. The endurance contraction should be built up to a 10-second contraction.

Type: The muscles in the pelvic floor have endurance (like a marathon), or quick (like a sprint), contraction ability. Doing both quick pulsing contractions and longer holds will train all the muscle types. Work what feels the weakest, but work out both types.

To work on endurance, first see how long you can hold this combination exercise of both closing and lifting. Test your muscle endurance by counting how long you can hold the contraction and how many repetitions of that hold you can do. The goal is 30 repetitions per day with a 10-second hold.

To work on quick pulsing contractions, rapidly tense both layers of muscles (one second) and release for two seconds. Focus on the movement of the clitoris and the closing of the vaginal opening. Repeat this 10 times in a row.

If the contractions are hard to do or you can't feel the muscle working, see a physical therapist that specializes in pelvic floor function and dysfunction to help you with your muscle-training program. The therapist can use biofeedback and other rehabilitation techniques to help you regain muscle strength and control.

Helpful hints to monitor yourself and to be sure you are exercising correctly.

- Use a mirror to see, or a finger to feel, if the muscles are puckering and pulling inward closing off the anus and the vagina. Observe the muscles moving the clitoris downward. This clitoral movement might not be visible if you are weak or swollen right after delivery. Don't give up; keep sending messages to the first-layer muscles to nod the clitoris and contract the vaginal opening. The tone you get from the muscle strength will enhance your sexual pleasure.

- When you contract the pelvic floor, sometimes you will feel a slight deep tension in your lower belly. It is OK to use the deep belly muscles as long as you are not bearing down and straining with the exercise.
- Since the muscles are inside your body, no one can tell you are doing the exercises or see this belly tension. If you are moving your pelvis, chest, or legs while doing the exercise and your partner can tell by watching you that you are doing the pelvic floor exercises, then you are exercising more muscles than you should be, or exercising the wrong muscles. You may need the help of a physical therapist to learn proper exercise technique.
- The exercises should not hurt. If you have pain, you should consider releasing breathing exercises or a Reverse Kegel. (See Tips 4 and 5.)

Finally, be present and pay attention to your body during the exercises. Eventually you can do these during sexual activity, so start now by thinking about your body and your intimate relationship with it and your partner. Pelvic floor exercise time is reserved for you, so don't make checklists in your head, redesign the ceiling color, or think about the baby in the next room. Your mood will help the exercises feel erotic rather than like work.

TIP 9: PELVIC FLOOR PLAY ™—BREATHING AND MOVEMENT TECHNIQUES TO ENHANCE SEXUAL DESIRE

Beyond building strength and awareness in the pelvic floor muscles, you can use breathing techniques and timed pelvic floor contractions (pelvic floor play) to build a conscious connection to your body. Making this conscious link is another step to complete pelvic floor rehabilitation after childbirth. These engaging methods help you stay present with your body's sensations and can enhance your mood for sexuality. These methods, based on Eastern traditions, are designed to be more arousing than relaxing. You can try these techniques before and during sexual activity.

There are three breathing techniques—circular breathing, energetic breathing, and rocking breathing—that focus on moving the breath through your body and can be done independently or in conjunction with pelvic floor exercises.

TECHNIQUE 1 – CIRCULAR BREATHING WITH PELVIC FLOOR CONTRACTION

The purpose of this exercise is to train your muscles to work with your breath during sexual activity. You can learn to coordinate your breathing with your pelvic floor. As you inhale, the pelvic floor muscles stay relaxed and open to receive, as you exhale, the pelvic floor contracts to give to your partner.

This conscious contraction of the pelvic floor muscles and breathing should include images of moving your breath. While inhaling slowly through your mouth and nose, imagine the breath dropping down in the front of your body back into the tailbone at the base of your spine, as the pelvic floor relaxes. While exhaling, imagine the breath moving up the back of your spine to the top of your head, as the pelvic floor contracts. Together, this pattern completes a circle of breath movement. The pace of breathing can start slowly, but the intention is to increase the rate of breaths per minute and focus on the inward movement of your pelvic floor muscles.

TECHNIQUE 2 – BODY-FOCUSED BREATHING

The focus points for this breathing technique are between your pelvic region and the top of your head. This breathing focuses on moving your breath upward in stages to specific body regions that are related to energy centers known as chakras. To move through the energy centers, use the circular breathing technique at each region.

Start with the pelvic region base and move upward through seven key regions. This is done with one breath cycle for each of the seven regions.

- The base of your spine near your tailbone and sitting bones, all the way to the bottom of your pelvis.
- The pelvic organ region, a few inches below your belly button.
- The area associated with your gut, the solar plexus, a few inches above your belly button.
- The area near the heart, behind your ribs and in the center of your chest.
- The throat region.
- The area between your eyes.
- The top of the head.

Repeat the sequence several times in a row increasing the pace of breathing and feeling free to make sounds as you exhale.

TECHNIQUE 3 – ROCKING BREATHING

This technique incorporates movements of the pelvic floor, hips, and back together with your breath. It is done while lying on your back. Repeat this breathing for 1–5 minutes continuously.

- Breathe in, letting your belly fill like a balloon, arching your back and keeping your pelvic floor relaxed.
- Breathe out and flatten your back (rocking the pelvis) while contracting the pelvic floor muscles.
- Add leg and hip motions by letting your knees open as you breathe in and close as you blow out.
- Imagine the legs moving like butterfly wings. Allow the breath and contractions to be erotic by visualizing positive sexual experiences.

PELVIC FLOOR PLAY™

Remember Emily's story at the beginning of the book? After learning to release her pelvic floor muscles and massage her scar from the vaginal delivery of her baby, I taught her to do pelvic floor activities specifically for sexual arousal and awareness. This type of exercise and activity is what I call pelvic floor play™.

"Mentally, I was armed with some helpful information from my PT sessions, which ultimately helped me achieve orgasm for the first time, post-partum. I was taught that I could actually move my clitoris using my pelvic floor muscles. Knowing how to use your pelvic floor muscles to enhance intercourse is something I highly recommend. 'Getting to know' my pelvic floor has allowed me to enjoy sex once again and read my body on a whole new level."

Another great way to focus on your body sensations is through awareness and use of your pelvic floor muscles during foreplay and sexual activity. As mentioned in Tip 8 regarding pelvic floor strengthening, **strong pelvic floor muscles improve sexual function. You don't have to be a superwoman with Olympic caliber muscles to do pelvic floor play. It's a matter of how and when you send contract and release messages to your muscles.** To simplify a complex system of nerve wiring, it is important to remember that we can learn to specifically control and feel any part of our bodies. But you have to activate the wiring system in order to get a response.

The main nerve that goes to the pelvic floor muscles and perineum is called the pudendal nerve. The pudendal nerve has matching left and right nerve pathways. That means you can use one side of your pelvic floor muscles and not the other, or have differences between the sides from nerve stretching or injury during childbirth. On each side the pudendal nerve has three branches that go to three specific perineal regions: one that goes to the region of the clitoris, one that goes to the perineal body and vaginal region, and one that goes to the anus. Each part that has a branch (going to it) can send and receive a message to the perineum and vulva. Try learning the specific nerve and muscle activation sequencing initially on your own and then use it as part of your sexual foreplay repertoire. A playful thing you can learn to do is to move your clitoris without touching it!

SPECIFIC PELVIC FLOOR PLAY™

Now it is time to have fun! Pelvic floor play is about engaging the pelvic floor muscles in specific movements for your enjoyment rather than for rehabilitation. These specific movements will help you feel not only your individual perineal and genital parts but also the pelvic floor muscles contract and release. Pelvic floor play is a practice of isolating and sending signals that contract muscles that attach to the perineal structures. Try at least 2–5 signals in a row to move or contract the same region. Be sure to let go and relax between signals. There are four specific areas to concentrate on with pelvic floor play. See Table 4 for specific regions and activation cues.

TABLE FOUR: SPECIFIC PELVIC FLOOR PLAY SUGGESTIONS

REGION	PART OF PERINEUM	ACTIVATION OR MOVEMENT CUE
Top of the vulva	clitoris	Moving the hood and glans downward, nodding action
Front	urethra	Shut off or slow the flow of urine
Middle	vagina and perineal body	Close the vaginal opening, lift at the center
Back	anus	Squeeze (wink) the opening shut

Also, there are sides to each of the regions. You can isolate a contraction of the left side in each of the regions, and then do the same with the right side.

Further pelvic floor play techniques include different sequences of your regional pelvic floor contractions. There are many combinations of front, middle, back, and top that you can perform; here are a few examples.

- Think of starting with an anal wink, then a clitoral nod, then a vaginal closing.
- Think of starting with a clitoral nod, then a vaginal closing, then an anal wink.
- Think of starting with vaginal closing, then an anal wink, then a clitoral nod.
- While sitting, focus on the two sitting bones touching the chair. Think of lifting your deepest layer on the left, then on the right. Pulse back and forth between the two sides.

You can also do these exercises during intercourse. This is one time I recommend you multitask, contracting and releasing with any type of penetration so that both you and your partner can feel increased pleasure.

You can also use the pelvic floor muscles in several different ways with any vaginal penetration once you are pain free. Be sure you have mastered pelvic floor release and that there is no pain with contracting the muscles. Pleasure is the goal with these varying methods that contract your pelvic floor muscles. Penetration can include entering into the vagina with a finger, dilator, wand, or penis.

- Release the muscles as your vagina is entered and tighten the muscles as it goes out.

- Once penetrated, contract around and against the body part or tool and release in a pulsing mode 5–10 times in a row.
- Imagine you are grabbing the body part or tool with your muscles and pulling it further in with penetration.
- Think of moving or nodding just the clitoris.

THE WHOLE PICTURE

Your sexual desire has a lot to do with what else is going on in your newly designed and unpredictable life with a child. The breathing techniques and suggestion of pelvic floor play activations are designed to help you focus on your body sensations and what your brain thinks about or imagines during foreplay and sexual activity.

It is important to focus on all your senses because what you hear, smell, and see also can affect your sexual mood. Try playing your favorite sensual music and burning scented candles. A photo of your favorite get-away or a picture that calms you could be placed where you can see it.

Remind yourself to take good care of yourself and your relationship. Taking a walk on your own or while pushing a stroller with the family can promote fitness and give you energy. Doing specific exercises for the belly and the pelvic floor will help the parts of your body that carried the greatest load (Tips 8 and 10). For your relationship, plan a date night, get a babysitter or talk and touch each other after the baby is asleep. Keep working on connecting and communicating with your partner. Talking about your sexual life, the best times you have experienced, and/or favorite sex positions can foster some desire and arousal.

It is rare that fatigue is not a factor in returning to sexual activity. I've heard stories where sexual desire was present but once the couple got to the bedroom and the covers on the bed were pulled back, sleep became easier than sexual interactions. Please consider staying out of the bedroom or at least not lying down until you are ready for sexual activity. This may mean trying some alternative positions for sexual intercourse. That includes in a chair or in a supported kneeling or hands and knees position. Also consider straddle positions for intercourse where the woman is on top and can control the depth of penetration into the vagina. Do some experimenting to determine if front or back vaginal entry is more comfortable. If you have discomfort consider trying a variety of activities or positions. Don't give up without trying all the options!

INVOLVING YOUR PARTNER

Involve your partner in the activities suggested throughout the book. They can help you perform the pelvic inventory, especially mapping the vaginal opening and internal parts of the vagina for any painful areas. When your partner knows exactly where you hurt and what makes it hurt, then the two of you together can work to stretch or release the area. Do this with the caveat of respecting where and what hurts you. Together you can work towards sexual fulfillment.

HERE ARE A FEW SEXUAL AROUSAL TECHNIQUES TO HELP YOU PREPARE FOR PENETRATION.

Prior to doing the external or internal stretching methods described in this book, consider adding sexual arousal techniques. This could involve anything that you know arouses you, including manually stimulating your clitoris. It could also include kissing, cuddling, spooning, and fondling, or whatever special intimacy you share with your partner. This foreplay does several things to prepare the body for vaginal penetration.

Sexual arousal and excitement cause an increase in blood flow and engorgement (known as vasocongestion) to the genital area. The vaginal tissues naturally lubricate in this engorged state. Sexual arousal also creates lubrication from the Bartholin's gland (see glossary of terms). This gland is located between the first and second layers of the pelvic floor muscles, so contracting and releasing these layers may enhance blood flow to the region. But be aware and remember that natural lubrication is often compromised during breastfeeding. If you are aroused and excited and drier than you expected to be, remember that this is a temporary post-partum body change. Use ample lubricant and review the types of lubricants available in Tip 3. Arousal will also cause the vagina to lengthen one to two inches in a process called "vaginal tenting," a response to excitement. This lengthening helps accommodate penetration. Vaginal size returns to its normal 3–4-inch length when it is unaroused.

TIP 10: RECLAIMING YOUR CORE—EXCERICISES FOR STRENGTHENING TRUNK MUSCLES AND MOVING ABDOMINAL SCARS

"My belly is so different after having my baby."

When you were pregnant, you experienced changes in your abdominal wall and trunk muscles as your muscles stretched to make room for the growing baby. It is natural for the abdomen to stretch during pregnancy. Many women accommodate and recover from this easily, while others experience lasting changes. In women who undergo a C-section delivery, scar tissue can form at the incision, leading to pulling, tightness, or pain in the scar. This section includes common tips and techniques to restore your abdominal wall after vaginal or C-section delivery.

Juanita came to see me with concerns about her belly appearance after the delivery of her first child. Luckily, she is not experiencing significant back or pelvic pain; she tells me she feels that her "six-pack abdominals have turned into a keg. I want to rebuild my core and feel sexy again." She is concerned about a separation of her belly muscles and the lack of tone and is wondering if she will regain her former body. She also recognizes that the way she feels about her body since the birth of her child inhibits her ability to let go and enjoy great sex.

First of all, you must accept that it takes time to recover from the changes all over your body from childbirth. One way to kill your sex drive is to judge yourself and your body too harshly. You don't have to be perfect to feel good about your body or have sexual desire. Every woman is unique in her recovery, and the changes in her belly and body are unique to her as well. In my experience almost every postpartum woman has universal interest in her belly strength, appearance, and one day recovering a strong "core." Sometimes the interest is immediate, sometimes it is delayed. Juanita was on the right track;

she was paying attention to her body and seeking care and treatment.

There is a combination of four muscle groups in the trunk that is referred to as the abdominal canister or inner core. This team of muscles is your internal girdle or corset of support for the spine, pelvis, and internal organs. It needs special recovery after childbirth. The muscles of the canister include the pelvic floor on the bottom, the transversus abdominis muscles in the front, the multifidi (the innermost lower back muscles) in the back, and the diaphragm (breathing) muscle on the top.

Figure 22 • The Four Muscles Groups of the Abdominal Canister or Inner Core

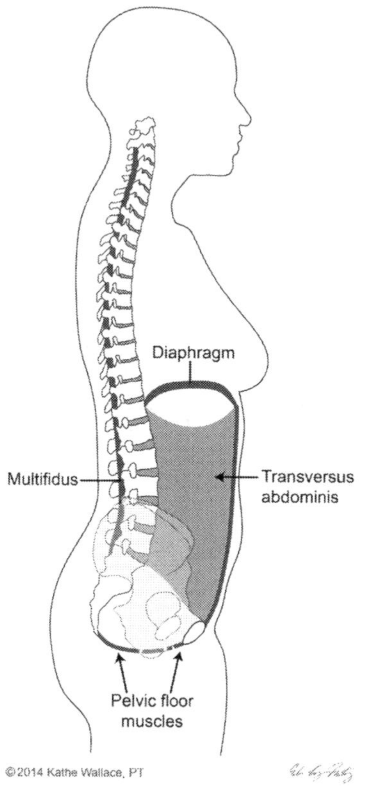

Let's learn more about the four inner core muscle group team members. These muscles surround the important organs and the spine, supporting the canister contents from front, back, top, and bottom.

- The bottom of the canister, the pelvic floor muscles, is described in Tip 8. These muscles are responsible for controlling and releasing the three openings in the bottom of the pelvis.
- The deepest abdominal muscle, the transversus abdominis, is the front abdominal muscle and wraps from side to side around the abdomen like a supportive belt, or girdle. When contracted, these muscles tense and flatten the lower and side-wall region of the belly narrowing your waistline.
- The deep back muscles, the multifidi, are the innermost back muscles and are positioned to support the spine and pelvis. These muscles act like the lacing on the back of a corset. When contracted, the tension generated by these muscles creates support for the front and back of the trunk.
- The top of the canister is the breathing muscle, or diaphragm. Using the diaphragm to control breathing affects the pressure of the canister. Coordination of breathing is important with exercise and daily activities.

These four muscle groups are the foundation of your core, and it is important to connect with these muscles and train them to work together. Working muscles together is called a co-contraction. Targeting your exercise to the inner core muscles will wake up and strengthen the stretched and weakened muscles involved with pregnancy and childbirth. It takes practice, concentration, and focus on the muscles to time and sequence the effort of your core from the inside. You must train them to activate before you strengthen them. This training exercise is called the core brace.

THE CORE BRACE EXERCISE: TRAINING THE KEY INSIDE MUSCLES OF YOUR TRUNK

Before your pregnancy you likely did this trunk muscle co-contraction automatically. After giving birth, these core muscles are not likely to recover quickly or at all without retraining the core brace muscles. This is not a maximal effort exercise but more a strategy of using your core. The complete inner core brace exercise involves working your pelvic floor, belly, and back muscles at the same time while breathing. The co-contraction creates muscle support for your pelvic contents, belly, back, and pelvic structures.

Position yourself on the floor or bed with your back slightly curved away from the floor. This is called the "neutral position." Placing your hand or a small rolled-up towel under your lower back helps maintain your neutral spine. The goal is to discourage pelvis and spine movement and avoid flattening your lower back to the floor with the exercise.

The goal is to activate the muscles during the core brace with a low level effort. Contract gradually and slowly, as if you are turning on a dimmer switch, using less than your maximum effort. Breathing should be focused on moving the rib cage rather than making the belly rise. You should continue to breathe moving your rib cage in and out while holding the contraction in the pelvic floor, transversus, and multifidi muscles. You will feel the tension of the core brace deep in the abdomen.

Start by holding the core brace for 5 seconds. Work up to 10 seconds. Repeat the contraction 10 times in a row. Keep breathing in and out during the contractions. You can continue to progress up to 30 contractions per day.

STEPS FOR ACTIVATING YOUR CORE BRACE MUSCLES

1. Focus on your pelvic floor muscles (Figure 21a and 21b) at the base of your pelvis. To contract them, imagine you are slowly shutting off the urine flow, partially holding back gas, and closing the vagina. This contraction creates tension around your bladder, anus, and vagina.

2. While you hold the pelvic floor contraction tension, add in the lower belly muscles (transversus abdominis) without moving your back or pelvis. Do this by imagining that your seat belt is wrapped firmly around your lower belly and is flattening or hollowing the belly wall. The transversus abdominis muscle will create a tension low and deep in the abdominal wall.

3. Finally, engage the multifidi, the deep back muscles, by tensing the muscles next to your spine. Find them by thinking of the muscles that create a slight arch in your low back. Imagine a zipper running from the tailbone and pelvis up to the rib cage. This will create support to the canister from the back.

Your inner thigh and buttock muscles like to help out if your core brace muscles are weak. That is very generous of these muscles, however, it does not help your core brace. Sometimes women report mid-back tension and breath-holding during the core brace. This is also from neighboring muscles trying to help out. If this is happening, you likely are tensing too hard.

The core muscles are needed to do skills throughout the day. Once you have mastered these exercises lying down, it is important to learn to use this core brace in multiple positions. Try the exercises in side-lying, sitting, and standing. You will be able to master the sense of tensing these core muscles prior to progressing to other exercises and functional activities. When you do begin other exercises, always use the core brace muscles first and keep your back in neutral with all of your traditional abdominal exercises. There are several ways to find the core muscles and progress your core brace. Suggestions are available at Kathewallace.com /book-resources.

Juanita learned to use her core brace muscles, and then was able to build on her exercise program. She says that while she may not have her six-pack back, her "keg" is gone and her core feels stronger, allowing her return to her active lifestyle. She also was proud of reclaiming her core muscles, and those changes made her feel empowered and sexy again.

DIASTASIS RECTUS ABDOMINIS

"My belly is so different after having my baby."

Diastasis rectus abdominis (DRA) is a separation of the abdominal muscles. It is a common condition during pregnancy and can persist after some pregnancies. The abdominal muscles and the linea alba, a connective tissue that connects the right and left abdominal muscles, can be overly stretched and impaired after childbirth. In some women, a diastasis rectus can prevent normal functioning of the core muscles. For others, the muscles still work, but the changed appearance of the belly can seem strange, uncomfortable, and unsexy. It is common to worry about the abdominal muscle separation and be fearful about starting an exercise program. Fear not, this section is designed to address your separation anxiety.

BELLY SEPARATIONS *(Also Called Diastasis Rectus Abdominis)*

About 30% of women have a diastasis rectus after childbirth. A diastasis can be many different widths. Whatever the width, it can be an emotionally distressing consequence of childbirth and might contribute to pelvic pain, back pain, or urinary incontinence. Recovery from a separation or diastasis can take several paths. In most women the separation heals spontaneously. It will narrow in the weeks following childbirth, and even if a separation does persist, it is minimal. The muscles and fascia still remain functional and support the core. If this is you, lucky you!

However, if the separation persists after eight weeks post-partum, the diastasis is unlikely to change without a specific program of core or trunk muscle training. If your recovery path also includes back or pelvic girdle pain that persists after childbirth, then the concern goes beyond the appearance of the abdomen and your sexual concerns. Between 5% and 7% of women will continue to have back or pelvic girdle pain for more than three months postpartum. While the pain is not always related to a diastasis (DRA), having a separation of the abdominal muscles can make it difficult to recruit and use the core muscles to stabilize the low back, trunk, and pelvis. An abdominal separation can also contribute to urinary incontinence, fecal incontinence, and prolapse of the organs.

Diane Lee, a Canadian physiotherapist and researcher in the area of rehabilitation of diastasis rectus abdominis, describes the problem as "an abdominal wall with a broken zipper that is unable to function properly." Preliminary studies to be published (Lee, D & Hodges, P W) indicate that the healthy abdominal wall is able to generate tension in the center of the belly (the area of the linea alba) during tasks that challenge the back and spine. This means a healthy abdominal wall works to create this tension while you lift your child out of a crib or put her in the car seat. In other words, your abdominal zipper stays closed.

The studies also identified two specific consequences that can occur when the separation persists. In the first scenario the post-partum belly is unable to generate this healthy tension because the muscles are not working together and turning on at the right time. This is called a non-optimal strategy. It is like trying to zip a zipper when the teeth aren't lined up. The other scenario occurs because of the anatomical changes from the separation (DRA). The fascia (the layers of complex connective tissue) that are designed to connect the abdominal muscles are stretched out. The anatomical changes represent a stretched zipper. Even if the muscles are working, they aren't trained yet to create enough tension in the fascia. Both types need a treatment program to retrain the zipper. On rare occasions, the tissue is too stretched for the muscles to be able to tense. In these situations, surgery for the DRA may be required to fix the zipper.

What is important when retraining a belly with DRA from either cause is that the core muscles learn to generate tension in the gap. The key area of focus for this tension recovery is in and along the zipper region from the bottom of the breast bone to the top of the pubic bone. Closing the gap (DRA) is less important for your functional recovery and pain reduction than being able to generate tension at the linea alba. In other words, you may still see a separation in your belly, but if you can feel tension in the fascia between the gap, your musculoskeletal back or pelvic girdle symptoms are usually improved.

Katie came to my office three months after delivering her first child. She is concerned about pain in her lower back, as well as a separation in her abdominal muscles. She tells me that she can fit "a couple fingers" in the gap below her belly button and that it feels "mushy" even when she tries to do a sit-up or plank. She also says that her lower back hurts when she lifts her 3-month-old baby out of his crib, when she plays on the floor with him, or when she takes his car seat in and out of the car. She's not interested in sex because she is in too much discomfort.

In Katie's case, there are two simple tests that will help determine if the diastasis rectus is contributing to her back problems. These are self-screening tests you can do at home to help determine whether or not a diastasis is a functional as well as an esthetic problem for you. The tests below are adapted from the brochure "Your Body after Baby," Physiotherapy Association of British Columbia, Canada.

SELF-SCREENING TESTS FOR DIASTASIS RECTUS ABDOMINIS

The Curl-Up Test: Lie on your back with your knees bent. Keeping your chin tucked in, slowly lift your head and shoulders up off the floor until your shoulder blades are no longer touching the floor. Assess your response by answering these questions:

- Do you have back, pubic, or pelvic pain with the movement?
- Do you see any bulging (like a mound) at the midline of your abdomen?
- Do you feel a separation or soft gap in the midline (at your belly button) between the borders of the rectus abdominis? Check along the middle of your belly from the arch of the rib cage to your pubic bone.

The Leg Lift Test: Lie on your back with your legs straight. Lift one leg up off the ground about two to four inches. Return it to the ground. Assess. Repeat with the other side. Assess your response by answering these questions:

- Do you have back, pubic, or pelvic pain with the movement?
- Do you see any bulging (like a mound) at the midline of your abdomen?
- Do you feel a separation or soft gap in the midline (at your belly button) between the borders of the rectus abdominis? Check along the middle of your belly from the arch of the rib cage to your pubic bone.

If your answer is yes to any of these symptoms, begin with the core brace exercise. Seek help from a physical therapist with experience in women's health and diastasis rehabilitation.

EXERCISE STRATEGY FOR A DIASTASIS RECTUS ABDOMINIS

If you have a diastasis, the rehabilitation of the core muscles is the key. Using proper technique and timing while training the core muscles will help you get stronger and you will be better able to use your core. Use the core brace exercise instructions described earlier. This means you will start by learning to tighten a team of muscles that contribute to the proper abdominal tension and activation: your pelvic floor muscles, your transversus abdominis, and the multifidi. Once you can connect with your inner core and activate the muscles, you will be able to use the right sequencing of muscles. This exercise strategy is the foundation you will build upon with other abdominal exercises. For example, perform a core brace prior to doing a squat or a standing abdominal exercise with a therapy ball or band. You can also begin to use your core brace in daily activities such as squatting and reaching.

Doing traditional sit-ups is not the answer to correcting a diastasis, and doing them improperly might make the diastasis wider. Instead, learn to use the inner canister muscles by doing a core brace. Once you can perform a core brace, you can use this as a foundation or "pre-contraction" before abdominal exercises.

Again, I encourage you to try the basic core brace exercise and to seek out a physical therapist if you don't feel like you are succeeding. They can perform a complete assessment of your posture, moving and lifting strategies as well as the myofascial and specific boney alignment in the muscles and joints of your post-partum body. From the assessment a specific exercise and treatment plan can be designed specifically for you. Sometimes temporary use of abdominal supports known as binders, belts, or braces will help the muscles remember to work. Supports can also help back or pelvic pain, but without a muscle activation strategy like the core brace the changes might not last.

In more extreme cases, if physical therapy and core brace training doesn't change your pain and body image, the diastasis can be surgically repaired. However, surgery should not be considered until you have attempted an exercise program for up to one year. Also, this surgery may not be covered by most insurance companies at this time. This might change in the future with more research into the rehabilitation of a diastasis rectus for pain, bowel, and bladder symptoms.

In Katie's case, once she learned to activate and use her deep core muscles, she began to tighten those muscles before lifting her baby out of his crib and before getting up and down off the floor. She became more aware of how she moved and began to use better body mechanics. By activating her core muscles before lifting, she avoided pain when she moved her baby's car seat. Her core muscles grew stronger. She still has a diastasis, but it doesn't feel "mushy" any more, and she is able to take care of her baby without pain.

THE ABDOMEN AFTER C-SECTION: SCAR TISSUE MASSAGE AND MOBILIZATION

Jessica came to see me three months after she had her baby by C-section. Since the delivery she can wear only her maternity clothes; any pants with zippers rub against her scar and hurt. She hasn't tried any exercise yet because of the discomfort and fear of doing exercises wrong. She's also worried about sex with her husband. She tells me they've tried to initiate sex a few times, but if anything touches her scar, even accidentally, it hurts and stops them. She wants things to "feel normal again," and misses the intimacy of sex.

Many women experience discomfort in their C-section scar even when the scar is healed and looks normal. Often anything that brushes up against the scar makes it feel uncomfortable. This certainly can discourage intimate touch and your desire for sexual activity. The scar can feel sore when you wear certain pants or underwear. Also, it might feel like you can't use your abdominal muscles like you used to. All of these problems may be caused by restricted mobility of the scar. This is known as an adhesion.

As the scar heals over a two-year period, it should flatten into a smooth white line. Scars usually itch as they heal, and they can have areas of numbness. Scars that get infected often have greater restrictions and adhesions. For the first few weeks after your C-Section, it is normal for a scar to appear pink or red and slightly raised. However, scars should not cause excessive discomfort or restriction of activity after the first few weeks. Call and visit your health care provider if something does not seem right to you.

Abdominal scar massage may not have been taught after your C-section. In my practice I perform and teach scar massage because my clients experience improved ability to activate and use the abdominal muscles. The movement gained with scar massage improves the muscle function, making it easier to exercise and strengthen muscles. Moving and massaging the scar adhesions can also decrease pain around the scar.

Abdominal scars can also cause adhesions that can limit the mobility of the pelvic organs. Specifically, when the bladder, uterus, or vagina have limited mobility in any direction, pain with deeper vaginal penetration and with thrusting can occur. Massaging the scar could restore this mobility.

There are two parts to abdominal scar massage. Stage one is desensitization and skin stretching, stage two is direct scar massage.

STAGE ONE: SCAR DESENSITIZATION AND SKIN STRETCHING.

Scar desensitization is used to help decrease the irritation in a scar. For some people, a scar can become hypersensitive, making it difficult to tolerate touch or pressure. Gentle scar-desensitization exercises and skin stretching may help calm overexcited nerve endings and decrease sensitivity. While additional research on scar massage in C-sections is needed, I regularly see improvements with these techniques in my clinical practice.

You can begin stage one six weeks after your surgery or later. Set aside 10–15 minutes per day for these massage techniques to help your scar feel, look, and move more normally. Always have clean hands with little to no lotion for these activities.

SCAR-DESENSITIZATION DIRECTIONS

- Contact the scar and skin around the scar with a wet hand towel or washcloth. See figure 23a.
- Make motions **up and down**, **side to side**, or in **circles** for 1 to 3 minutes in order to get the scar used to being touched.
- Do this **daily** after bathing until there is no sensitivity to touching the scar with the hand towel or washcloth.

Figure 23a • Desensitization with a Hand Towel

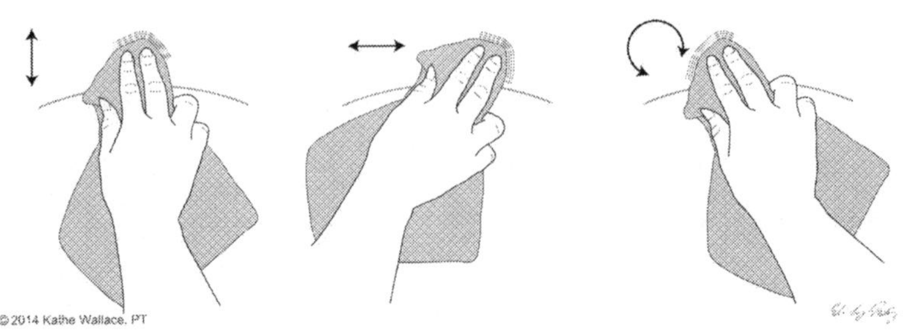

If you find areas that are more sensitive, work those spots with 5 to 10 more motions of the wet washcloth or hand towel.

Once you are comfortable with the hand towel, you can try gently rubbing the scar with different materials. Try using a soft blanket, a rough blanket, a sponge or loofah in the shower, a child's soft hairbrush, or a stuffed animal. You can find different materials around the house. Just be careful not to use anything sharp or painful.

SKIN-STRETCHING TECHNIQUES

Begin with light pressure in your fingertips. Over time, try applying different depths of pressure. Do not apply maximum pressure around your scar. It is normal to feel a pull or light burning when stretching around the scar. If you feel an area that does not move easily, or is extra sensitive, do a few more skin stretches over that area.

SKIN-STRETCHING DIRECTIONS

- Place your fingers 2 to 3 inches from your scar.
- Stretch the skin around the scar area by moving your fingers **up and down**. Make up-and-down motions around the entire scar.
- Stretch the skin around the scar area by moving your fingers **side to side**. Make side-to-side motions around the entire scar.
- Stretch the skin by making **circles** above and below the scar in a **clockwise** and **counterclockwise** direction. Make circular motions around the entire scar.
- Repeat each pattern 5 to 10 times.

Figure 23b • Skin Stretching Using Fingers

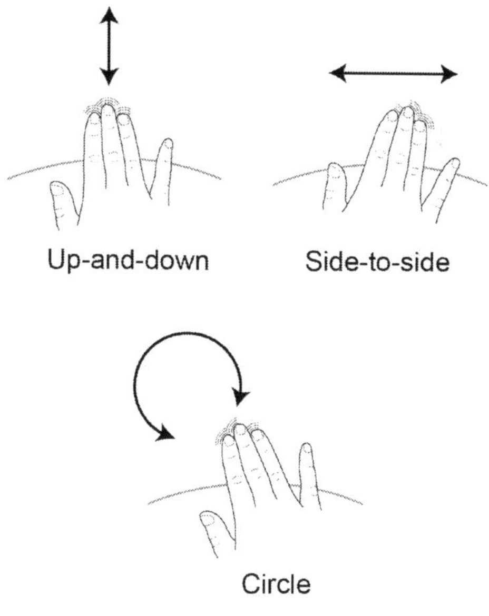

STAGE TWO: DIRECT SCAR STRETCHING.

Recent studies on skin tissue show that stretching skin scars limits excessive scarring. This research may explain why clinicians who perform scar massage find that their clients have improved scar healing. In addition, several clinical studies show that massage to a scar can improve the movement and decrease how noticeable the scar seems.

You can begin stage two twelve weeks after your surgery or later. Set aside 5 to 10 minutes for each session of scar stretching and scar lift and roll. Gradually progress the massage toward using firmer pressure when doing scar stretching and scar lift and roll. To get maximum mobility, do the techniques listed while you are performing your core brace. Contracting the muscles around the scar could also help the entire abdominal wall and its contents move better.

SPECIFIC SCAR-STRETCHING DIRECTIONS

These steps apply to three separate movements of the scar: side to side, up and down, and diagonal. See Figures 25, 26 and 27.

- Hold the pads of two or three fingers together. The fingers should be slightly arched, as shown in Figure 24. This finger and hand positioning is specific to scar stretching.
- Place the pads of your fingers directly on one end of the scar.
- Stretch the scar by pushing your fingers about half an inch in one direction as indicated by the black arrow. Hold the scar stretched for 5–15 seconds.

- Now stretch the scar opposite to the direction in step 3. Hold the scar stretched for 5–15 seconds.
- Move over to the next area of your scar and repeat the scar stretches as above. Work your way along the entire length of the scar.
- Repeat from 5 to 10 passes along the scar.

Figure 24 • Hand Positioning

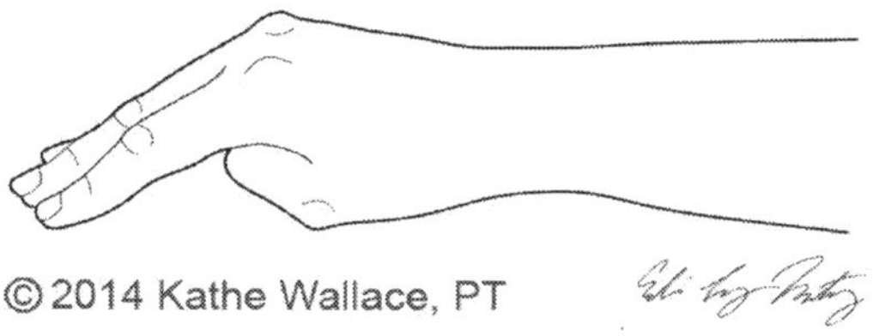

©2014 Kathe Wallace, PT

Figure 25 • Side-to-Side Stretching

©2014 Kathe Wallace, PT

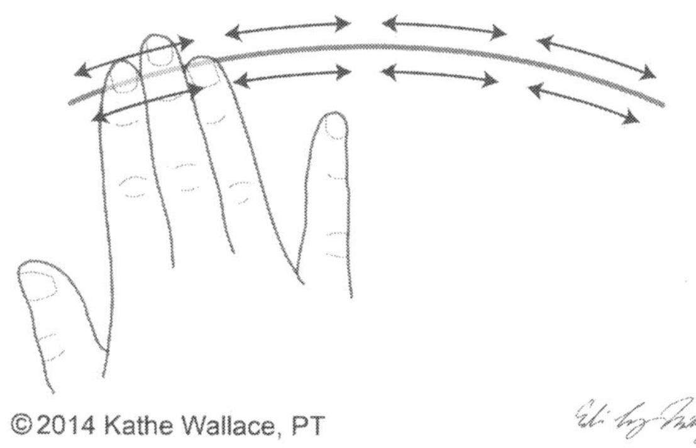

Figure 26 • Up-and-Down Stretching

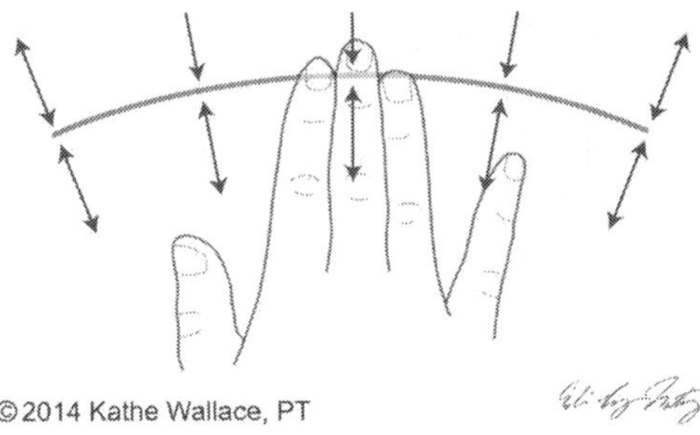

Figure 27 • Diagonal Stretches

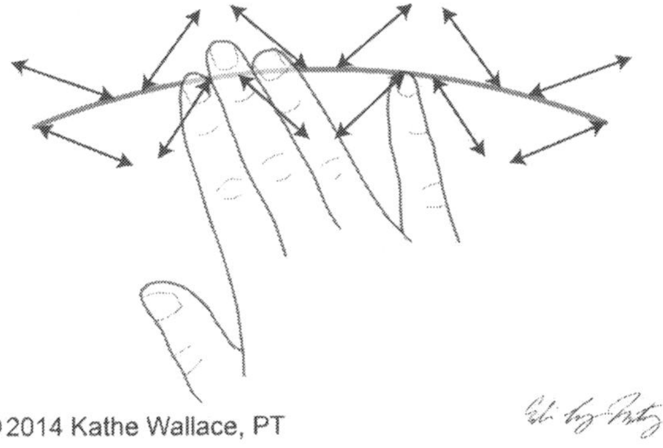

SCAR LIFT AND ROLL DIRECTIONS

- Pick up the scar between your index finger and thumb as shown in Figure 28.
- Roll the scar between your fingers for 5–15 seconds.
- Move along the scar and repeat until you have massaged the entire length of the scar.

Figure 28 • Scar Lift and Roll

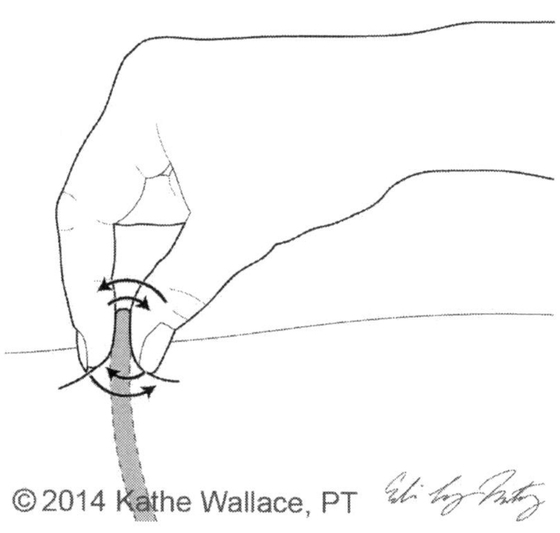

I began treatment for Jessica by doing gentle scar desensitization exercises. She noticed a decrease in sensitivity within the first week. She progressed gradually to working on scar massage, as well as doing her core bracing exercises. Her scar is still healing, but she is back in her regular clothes and enjoying her husband's touch.

SUMMARY

You now know how your body works after childbirth and have simple tools, tips, and techniques for what your body needs. These were designed to shorten your sexual recovery process. I encourage you to reunite with who you are sexually and remember that a mother can be sexy. The process of pregnancy and birth can be a challenge to your body and your sexuality. These first steps are simple tips and don't require medications or surgery, providing a natural first step to reviving your pelvic floor and your sexuality. Enjoy the process and the results!

There are other medical conditions that cause trigger points, tender or weak muscles, or painful intercourse or touch. If you are having persistent problems after trying these basic techniques, you may have problems that are more medical than musculoskeletal. See your women's health care provider and seek evaluation and treatment for your condition. This is not an exhaustive description of what physical therapy or medical providers have to offer post-partum women or women with pelvic pain that interferes with sexual function. Experts acknowledge that sexual function is complex and many factors play a role in changes in function during the post-partum period.

Getting help with sexual problems requires you to sometimes go beyond your comfort zone by asking for and getting the help you need to enjoy sex again.

SOME RESOURCES FOR WOMEN

Carter, M., & Carter, L. (2004). *Completely Overcome Vaginismus: Personal Journal & Workbook*. Canada: Vaginismus.com.

Carter, M., & Carter, L. (2004). *Completely Overcome Vaginismus: The Practical Approach to Pain-Free Intercourse*. Canada: Vaginismus.com.

Coady, D., & Fish, N. (2011). *Healing Painful Sex, a Woman's Guide to Confronting, Diagnosing, and Treating Sexual Pain*. CA: Seal Press.

Goldstein, A., Pukall, C., & Goldstein, I. (2011). *When Sex Hurts, A Woman's Guide to Banishing Sexual Pain*. Cambridge, MA: Da Capo Lifelong.

Herrera, I. (2009*). Ending Female Pain, a Woman's Manual, Ultimate Self-Help Guide for Women Suffering from Chronic Pelvic and Sexual Pain*. New York, NY: Duplex Publishing.

Perelli, K., & Kassai, K. (2011). *The Bathroom Key, Put an End to Incontinence*. New York, NY: Demos Medical Publishing.

Pirie, A. and Herman, H. (2003).*How to Raise Children without Breaking Your Back*. 2nd Edition. Somerville, MA, IBIS Publications.

Stein, A. (2008). *Heal Pelvic Pain: The Proven Stretching, Strengthening, and Nutrition Program for Relieving Pain, Incontinence,& IBS, and Other Symptoms Without Surgery*. New York, NY: McGraw-Hill.

Stewart, E.G., & Spencer, P. (2002). *The V Book*. New York, NY: Bantam Books.

PELVIC FLOOR PRODUCTS

Kathewallace.com /book-resources

WEBSITES ON SEXUALITY

sexualityresources.com

sexualrehab.com

tallirosenbaum.com

sexualmed.org

FINDING A WOMEN'S HEALTH PHYSICAL THERAPIST

womenshealthapta.org/pt-locator/

hermanwallace.com/practitioner-directory

ioptwh.org/members/members.cfm

REFERENCES

GLOSSARY

Clemente, C. (1997). *Clemente anatomy: A regional atlas of the human body.* (4th ed.): Williams & Wilkins.

Drake, R. (2010). *Gray's anatomy for students.* Philadelphia, PA: Elsevier/Churchill Livingstone.

Snell, R. (1995). *Clinical anatomy for medical students.* (5th ed.): Boston: Little Brown.

OVERVIEW: HOW CHILDBIRTH CHANGES YOUR BODY AND CHALLENGES YOUR SEXUALITY. WHAT HAPPENS TO MAKE IT CHANGE?

Abdool, Z., Thakar, R., & Sultan, A.H. (2009). Postpartum female sexual function. *European Journal of Obstetrics & Gynecology and Reprodroductive Biology, 145*(2), 133-7.
Acele, E.Ö., & Karaçam, Z. (2012). Sexual problems in women during the first postpartum year and related conditions. *Journal of Clinical Nursing, 21*(7-8), 929-37.

Bertozzi, S., Londero, A., Fruscalzo, A., Driul, L., & Marchesoni, D. (2010). Prevalence and risk factors for dyspareunia and unsatisfying sexual relationships in a cohort of primiparous and secondiparous women after 12 months postpartum. *International Journal of Sexual Health,* 22(1), 47-53.

Bump, R.C., & Norton, P. (1998). Epidemiology and natural history of pelvic floor dysfunction. *Obstetrics & Gynecology Clinics of North America, 25,* 723–746.

DeLancey, J.O. (2002). Fascial and muscular abnormalities in women with urethral hypermobility and anterior vaginal wall prolapse. *American Journal of Obstetrics & Gynecology, 187*(1), 93-8.

Fonti,Y., Giordano, R., Cacciatore, A., Romano, M., Larosa, B. (2009) Post-partum pelvic floor changes. *J Prenat Med.*3(4):57-9.

Handa, V.L., Cundiff, G., Chang, H.H., & Helzlsouer, K.J. (2008). Female sexual function and pelvic floor disorders. *Obstetrics & Gynecology, 111*(5), 1045-52.

Hagen. S., Stark D. (2011). Conservative prevention and management of pelvic organ prolapse in women. *Cochrane Database Syst Rev.* 12:CD003882.

Hicks, T.L., Goodall, S.F., Quattrone, E.M., & Lydon-Rochelle, M.T. (2004). Postpartum sexual functioning and method of delivery: summary of the evidence. *Journal of Midwifery and Women's Health, 49*(5), 430-6.

Leeman, L.M. (2012). Sex after childbirth: postpartum sexual function. *Obstetrics & Gynecology, 119*(3), 647-55.

Macarthur, A.J., & Macarthur, C. (2004). Incidence, severity, and determinants of perineal pain after vaginal delivery: a prospective cohort study. *American Journal of Obstetrics & Gynecology, 191*(4), 1199-204.

Memon, H.U., & Handa, V.L. (2013). Vaginal childbirth and pelvic floor disorders. *Womens Health (Lond Engl), 9*(3), 265-77.

Morin, M., Bergeron, S. (2009). Pelvic floor rehabilitation in the treatment of dyspareunia in women. *Sexologies, 18,* 91-94.

Mouritsen, L. (2009). Pathophysiology of sexual dysfunction as related to pelvic floor disorders. *InternationalUrogynecology Journal and Pelvic Floor Dysfunction, 1*, S19-25.

Persico, G., Vergani, P., Cestaro, C., Grandolfo, M., & Nespoli, A. (2013). Assessment of postpartum perineal pain after vaginal delivery: prevalence, severity and determinants. A prospective observational study. *Minerva Ginecologica, 65*(6), 669-78

Rathfisch, G. (2010). Effects of perineal trauma on postpartum sexual function. *Journal of Advanced Nursing, 66*(12), 2640-9

Rosenbaum, T. (2007). Pelvic Floor Involvement in Male and Female Sexual Dysfunction and the Role of Pelvic Floor Rehabilitation in Treatment: A Literature Review. *International Society for Sexual Medicine* 4: 4-13.

Rosenbaum, T. (2008). The Role of Physical Therapy in Female Sexual Dysfunction. *Current Sexual Health Reports,* 5: 97-101.

Serati, M., Salvatore, S., Siesto, G., Cattoni, E., Zanirato, M., Khullar, V. Bolis, P. (2010). Female sexual function during pregnancy and after childbirth. *The Journal of Sexual Medicine, 7*(8), 2782-90.

Sung, V. & Hampton, B. (2009). Epidemiology of pelvic floor dysfunction. *Obstetrics and Gynecology Clinics of North America, 36*(3), 421-43

Von Sydow, K. (1999). Sexuality during pregnancy and after childbirth: A metacontent analysis of 59 studies. *Journal of Psychosomatic Research, 47*(1), 27-49.

1. WASH, CARE AND WEAR—YOUR PERINEUM AFTER BIRTH AND BEYOND

American College of Nurse-Midwives. (2012). Vulvar Care. *Journal of Midwifery & Women's Health, 57*(3), 311-31. Retrieved from www.midwife.org/ACNM/files/cc

LibraryFiles/Filename/000000002192/Vulvar%20Care.pd

Majerovich, J.A., Canty, A., & Miedema, B. (2010). Chronic vulvar irritation: could toilet paper be the culprit?. *Canadian Family Physician, 56*(4), 350-2.

National Vulvodynia Association. (2013). *Self help tips for vulvar skin care*. Retrieved from - https://www.nva.org/Self_HelpTips.html

UpToDate. (2014). [Table of healthy vulvar hygeine practices]. Retrieved from http://www.uptodate.com/contents/im age? imageKey=OBGYN/64538&topicKey=OBGYN/5412& source=preview&rank=undefined

2. YOUR PELVIC ROSTER—PERSONAL INVENTORY CHECK

Carter, M., & Carter, L. (2004). *Completely Overcome Vaginismus*. Canada: Vaginismus.com.

Vulvar Anatomy. Available at: http://www.nva.org/vulvar Anatomy.html

3. DRY AND PAINFUL PARTS—VAGINAL LUBRICATION AFTER CHILDBIRTH

Herbenick, D., Reece, M., Schick, V., Sanders, S.A., Fortenberry, JD. (2014) Women's Use and Perceptions of Commercial Lubricants: Prevalence and Characteristics in a Nationally Representative Sample of American Adults. *The Journal of Sexual Medicine,* 11(3):642-52.

Sutton, K., Boyer, S., Goldfinger, C., Ezer, P., & Pukall, C. (2012). To lube or not to lube: experiences and perceptions of lubri cant use in women with and without dyspareunia. *The Journal of Sexual Medicine, 9*(1), 240-250.

4. LETTING GO—RELAX-AND-RELEASE BREATHING

Busch, V., Magerl, W., Kern, U., Haas, J., Hajak, G., Eichhammer ,P. (2012) The effect of deep and slow breathing on pain perception, autonomic activity, and mood processing--an experimental study. *Pain Medicine.13(2):*215-28.

5. IT HURTS BEFORE YOU START—EXERCISES TO RELEASE THE PELVIC FLOOR

Faubion, S.S., Shuster L.T., Bharucha, A.E. (2012) Recognition and management of nonrelaxing pelvic floor dysfunction. *Mayo Clin Proc. 87*(2):187-93.

FitzGerald, M.P., Kotarinos R. (2003) II: Rehabilitation of the short pelvic floor.Treatment of the patient with the short pelvic floor. *Int Urogynecol J Pelvic Floor Dysfunct*. 14:269.

Stein, A. (2008). *Heal Pelvic Pain: The Proven Stretching, Strengthen ing, and Nutrition Program for Relieving Pain, Inconti- nence,& IBS, and Other Symptoms Without Surgery*. New York, NY: McGraw-Hill.

http://www.uptodate.com/contents/pelvic-floor-physical-ther apy-for-management-of-myofascial-pelvic-pain-syn drome-in-women/abstract/3?utdPopup=true

6. WHAT TO DO IF YOU TORE DURING DELIVERY—WORKING WITH AN EPISIOTOMY OR PERINEAL TEARS

Best, T.M., Gharaibeh, B., Huard, J. (2013) Stem cells, angiogenesis and muscle healing: a potential role in massage thera pies? *Br J Sports Med.* 47(9): 556-60.

Herman, H. (2006). Physical therapy for female sexual dysfunc- tion. In: I. Goldstein, C. Meston, S. Davis, & A. Traish, (Eds.), Women's *Sexual Function And Dysfunction, Study,*

Diagnosis and Treatment. United Kingdom: Taylor & Francis.

Lewit, K., Olsanske, S. (2004). Clinical Importance of active scars: abnormal scars as and the cause of myofacial pain. *J Manipulative Physiol Ther.* 27: 399-402.

Rosenbaum, T.Y. (2005). Physiotherapy treatment of sexual pain disorders. *Journal of Sex and Marital Therapy, 31(4)*, 329-40.

7. WHEN IT HURTS WITH PENETRATION—INTERNAL STRETCH ING OF THE VAGINA AND PELVIC FLOOR MUSCLES, INCLUDING TRIGGER POINT AND SCAR TISSUE RELEASE

Anderson, R., Wise, D., Sawyer, T., & Nathanson, B.H. (2011). Safety and effectiveness of an internal pelvic myofascial trigger point wand for urologic chronic pelvic pain syndrome. *Clinical Journal of Pain, 27*(9), 764-8.

Dommerholt, J., Bron, C., et al. (2006). Myofascial Trigger Points: An Evidence-Informed Review. *The Journal of Manual & Manipulative Therapy*. 14 (4): 203 - 221.

Pastore, E.A., & Katzman, W.B. (2012). Recognizing myofascial pelvic pain in the female patient with chronic pelvic pain. *Journal of Obstetric, Gynecologic and Neonatal Nursing*. doi: 10.1111/j.1552-6909.Simons, D.G., Travell,

J.G., & Simons, L.S. (1999). *Travell & Simons' Myofascial Pain and Dysfunction : The Trigger Point Manual*. Philidelphia, PA: Lippincott Williams & Wilkins.

Simons, D.G., Dommerholt, J. (2006) Myofascial Trigger Points: An Evidence-Informed Review. *The Journal of Manual & Manipulative Therapy. 14(4), E124- E171*

Wise, D. & Anderson, R.U. (2011). *A Headache in the Pelvis: A new understanding and treatment for prostatitis and chronic pelvic pain syndromes*. Sixth Edition. Occidental, CA: National Center for Pelvic Pain Research.

8. FEELING LOOSE OR DIFFERENT IN THE VAGINA STRENGTH-ENING PELVIC FLOOR MUSCLES

Bø, K., & Talseth, T. (1996). Long-term effect of pelvic floor muscle exercise 5 years after cessation of organized training. *Obstetrics & Gynecology, 87*(2), 261-265.

Bump, R.C., Hurt, W.G., Fantl, J.A., Wyman, J.F. (1991). Assessment of Kegel pelvic muscle performance after brief verbal instruction. *American Journal of Obstetrics & Gynecology, 165*, 322-329

Fisher, K., & Riolo, L. (2004). What is the evidence regarding specific methods of pelvic floor exercise for a patient with urinary stress incontinence and mild anterior vaginal wall prolapse? *Physical Therapy, 84*(8), 744-753.

Kegel, A.H. (1949). The physiologic treatment of poor tone and function of the genital muscles and of urinary stress incontinence. *Western Journal of Surgery, Obstetrics, and Gynecology, 57*(11), 527-535.

Kegel, A.H. (1952). Sexual functions of the pubococcygeal muscle.*Western Journal of Surgery, Obstetrics, and Gynecology 60*(10), 521-524.

Miller, J.M. (2002). Criteria for therapeutic use of pelvic floor muscle training in women. *Journal of Wound Ostomy & Continence Nursing, 29*, 301-11.

9. PELVIC FLOOR PLAY TM—BREATHING AND MOVEMENT TECHNIQUES TO ENHANCE SEXUAL DESIRE

Cia, M. (2005). *Healing Love Through the Tao: Cultivating Female Sexual Energy*. Destiny Books.

Hendricks, G. (1995). *Conscious Breathing*. Bantam Books.

Meston, C. (2000). Sympathetic Nervous System Activity and Female Sexual Arousal. *American Journal of Cardiology,86*, 30f-34f.

Mullen, S. (2004). *The Best You'll Ever Have: What Every Woman Should Know About Getting and Giving Knock-Your-Socks-Off Sex*. New York, NY: Roundtable Press

Trudel, G & Saint-Laurent, S. (1983). A comparison between the effects of Kegel's exercises and a combination of sexual awareness relaxation and breathing on situational orgasmic dysfunction in women. *Journal of Sex & Marital Therapy, 9*(3), 204-9.

Tunneshende, M. (2001). *Don Juan and the Art of Sexual Energy: The Rainbow Serpent of the Toltecs*. Rochester, VT: Bear & Co. Voigt, H. (1991). Enriching the sexual experience of couples: the Asian traditions and sexual counseling. *Journal of Sex & Marital Therapy, 17*(3), 214-9.

10. RECLAIMING YOUR CORE—EXERCISES FOR STRENGTHENING TRUNK MUSCLES AND MOVING ABDOMINAL SCARS

Agha, R., Ogawa, R., Pietramaggiori, G., Orgill, D.P. (2011) A review of the role of mechanical forces in cutaneous wound healing. *Journal of Surgical Research. 2011; 171*(2): 700-708.

Arung, W., Meurisse, M., Detry O. (2011) Pathophysiology and prevention of postoperative peritoneal adhesions. World J Gastroenterol. 17(41): 4545-4553.

Benjamin, D.R., Van de water A.T., Peiris C.L. (2014). Effects of exercise on diastasis of the rectus abdominis muscle in the antenatal and postnatal periods: a systematic review. *Physiotherapy.* 100(1):1-8.

Bo, K., Sherburn, M., & Allen, T. (2003). Transabdominal ultrasound measurement of pelvic floor muscle activity when activated directly or via a transversus abdominis muscle contraction. *Neurourology and Urodynamics, 22*, 582-588.

Boissonnault, J.S., Blaschak, M.J. (1988). Incidence of diastasis recti abdominis during the childbearing year. *Phys Therapy,* 68(7):1082-6.

Coldron, Y., Stokes, M.J., Newham, D.J., & Cook, K. (2008). Postpartum characteristics of rectus abdominis on ultrasound imaging. *Manual Therapy, 13*(2), 112-21

Critchley, D. (2002). Instructing pelvic floor contraction facilitates transversus abdominis thickness increase during lower abdominal hollowing. *Physiotherapy Research International, 7*(2), 65-75.

Lee, Diane personal communications, December, 2013

Lee, D., Lee L.J., & McLaughlin, L. (2008). Stability, continence and breathing: The role of the fascia following pregnancy and delivery. *Journal of Bodywork and Movement Therapies, 12*(4), 333-48.

Mens, J., Vleeming, A., Snijders, C.J., Koes, B.W., & Stam, H.J. (2001). Reliability and validity of the active straight leg raise test in posterior pelvic pain since pregnancy. *Spine, 26*, 1167-71

Mens, J., Vleeming, A., Snijders, C.J., Ronchetti, I., Ginai, A.Z., & Stam, H.J. (2002). Responsiveness of outcome measurements in rehabilitation of patients with posterior pelvic pain since pregnancy. *Spine, 27*(10), 1110-1115.

Pool-Goudzwaard, A., Van Dijke, G.H., Van Gurp, M., Mulder, P., Snijders, C., & Stoeckart, R. (2004). Contribution of Pelvic Floor Muscles to Stiffness of the Pelvic Ring. *Clinical Biomechanics, 19*, 564-571.

Rath, A.M., Attali, P., Dumas, J.L., Goldlust, D., Zhang, J., Chevrel, J.P. (1996). The abdominal linea alba: an anatomo-radiologic and biomechanical study. *Surgical Radiologic Anatomy, 18*, 281–288.

Solcumb, J.C. (1993) Chronic somatic, myofascial and neurogenic abdominal pelvic pain. *Clinical Obstetrics and Gynecology,11* (1), 145-153

Spitznagle, T.M., Leong, F.C., & van Dillen, L.R. (2007). Prevalence of diastasis recti abdominis in a urogynecological patient population. *International Urogynecology Journal, 18*(3), 321-8.

PELVIC FLOOR AND PELVIC GIRDLE BOOKS

Calais-Germain, B. (2003). *The Female Pelvis: Anatomy & Exercise*. Seattle, WA: Eastland Press.

Carriere, B. & Feldt, C.M. (2006). *The Pelvic Floor*. New York, NY: Thieme.

Carriere, B. (2002). *Fitness for the Pelvic Floor*. New York, NY: Thieme.

Irion, J., Irion, G. (2010). *Women's Health in Physical Therapy*. Philidelphia, PA: Lippincott Williams and Wilkins.

Laycock, J, & Haslam, J. (2002). *Therapeutic management of incontinence and pelvic pain: pelvic organ disorders*. London, England: Springer-Verlag.

Lee, D. (2011). *The Pelvic Girdle: An Integration of Clinical Expertise and Research*. Philadelphia, PA: Churchill Livingstone.

Richardson, C. & Hodges, P. (1999). *Therapeutic Exercise for the Spinal Segmental Stabilization in Low Back Pain. Scientific Basis and Clinical Approach*. Philadelphia, PA: Churchill Livingstone.

Sapsford, R., Bullock-Saxton, J., Markwell, S. (1998). *Women's Health: A Textbook for Physiotherapists*. London, England: WB Saunders Co.

Simons, D.G., Travell, J.G., & Simons, L.S. (1999). *Travell & Simons' Myofascial Pain and Dysfunction : The Trigger Point Manual*. Philidelphia, PA: Lippincott Williams & Wilkins.

Wise, D. & Anderson, R.U. (2011). *A Headache in the Pelvis: A new understanding and treatment for prostatitis and chronic pelvic pain syndromes*. Sixth Edition. Occidental, CA: National Center for Pelvic Pain Research.

APPENDIX

PELVIC FLOOR AND WALL MUSCLES

There are 3 layers and 14 muscles in total that support the bottom and side walls of the pelvis. Their specific attachments, known as origins (O) and insertions (I), are outlined here.

Superficial Perineal Pouch: aka Surface Layer 1

These muscles are sphincters (close-off openings) with varying functions, such as closing and opening the bladder, bowel, and vaginal outlets, as well as moving the surrounding skin and clitoris. See figure 29.

Deep Perineal Pouch: aka Middle Layer 2

These muscles are sphincters (close-off openings) with functions specific to the bladder and vagina. See figure 29.

Pelvic Diaphragm: aka Deepest Layer 3 of the Pelvic Floor and the Side Walls

These muscles form a sling of support called the pelvic diaphragm, which supports the vagina, rectum and internal organ positions. See figure 30.

LAYER 1 – SUPERFICIAL PERINEAL POUCH
Superficial Transverse Perineal Muscle O: Ischial tuberosity I: Perineal body
Bulbocavernosus (Bulbospongiosus) O: Perineal body, travels under the labia I: Fascia of the corpus cavernosum of the clitoris
Ischiocavernosus O: Ischial tuberosity and ramus I: Inferolateral aponeurosis over crura of clitoris
External Anal Sphincter O: Perineal body and anal canal I: Coccyx
LAYER 2 – DEEP PERINEAL POUCH
External Urethral Sphincter O: Inferior pubic arch I: Blends with the anterolateral walls of the vagina and into the trigonal ring surrounding the urethra
Urethrovaginal Sphincter O: Vaginal wall I: Ventral surface of the urethra
Compressor Urethrae O: Ischiopubic ramus I: Vaginal wall
Deep Transverse Perineal O: Inner surface of the rami of the ischium I: Runs across to attach to opposite side

LAYER 3 – PELVIC DIAPHRAGM and SIDE WALLS
Pubococcygeus (Pubovisceral, Pubovaginalis) O: Dorsal surface of the pubic bone and fascia of the obturator internus I: Anococcygeal body, between the tip of the coccyx and the anal canal
Puborectalis O: Dorsal surface of the pubic bone and fascia of the obturator internus I: Anococcygeal body, sling around junction of rectum and anal canal
Iliococcygeus O: Arcus tendinous levator ani (a fibrous band suspended between the pubic bone and ischial spine) I: Anococcygeal body and the coccyx
Coccygeus (Ischiococcygeus) O: Arises from the spine of the ischium I: On the caudal portion of the sacrum and coccyx
Obturator Internus O: Internal or pelvic surface of the obturator foramen I: Medial surface of the greater trochanter of the femur proximal to the trochanteric fossa
Piriformis O: Pelvic surface of the sacrum, passes through the greater sciatic foramen I: Superior border of the greater trochanter of the femur

Figure 29 • Outer View Split Image of Pelvic Floor Muscle Layers with Muscle Identified

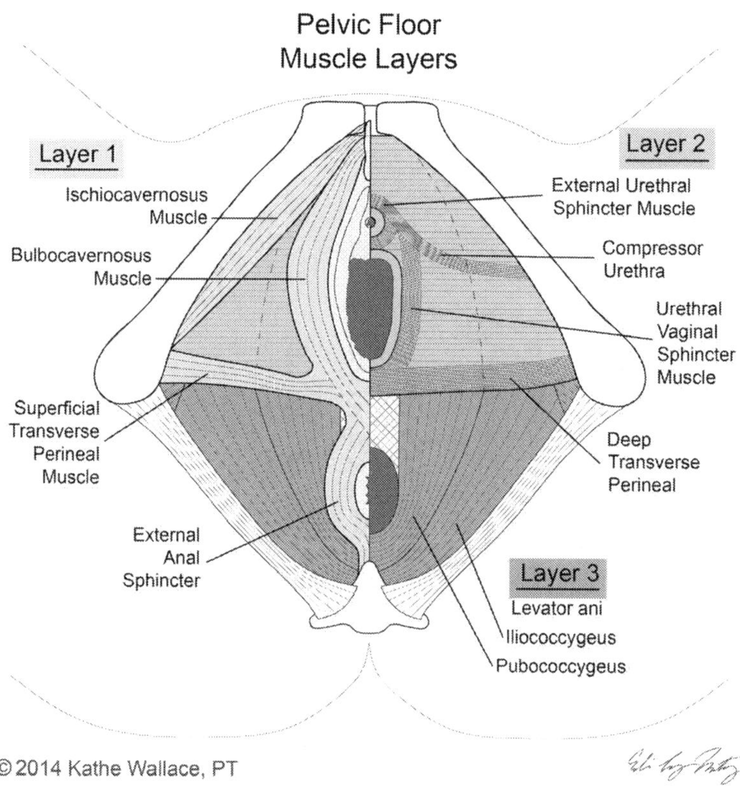

Figure 30 • Inside View (from above) of the Pelvic Floor Layer 3 with Muscle Identified

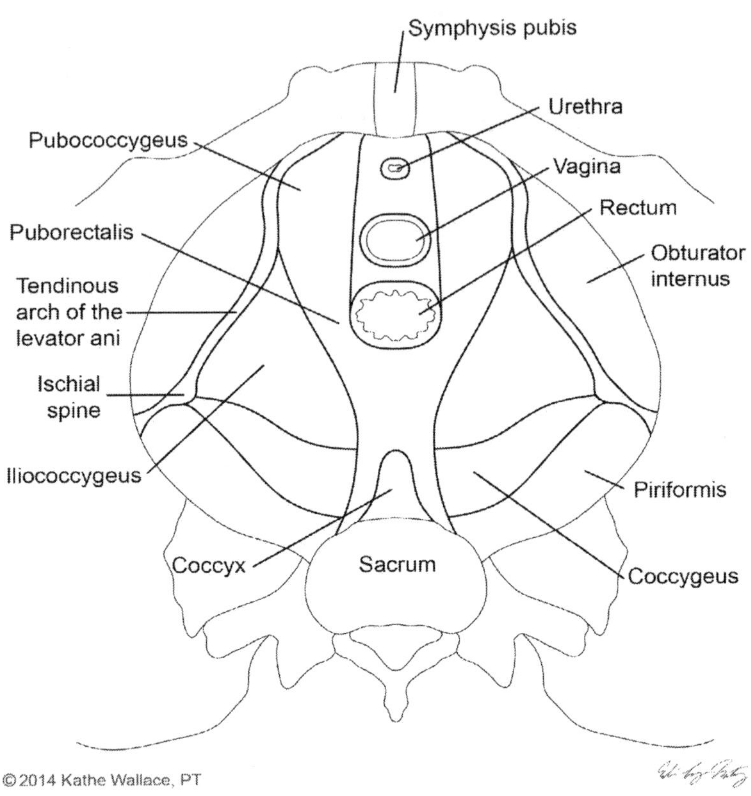

ABOUT THE AUTHOR

Kathe Wallace, PT, BCB-PMD, has practiced physical therapy since 1976. She is board certified through the Biofeedback Certification International Alliance in the treatment of Pelvic Muscle Dysfunction (BCB-PMD). As a nationally recognized pioneer and leader in the pelvic floor specialty of physical therapy, she evaluates and treats sexual function, bladder and bowel conditions, and through her treatment, she helps patients improve their quality of life.

In 1990, Kathe began teaching other physical therapists how to evaluate and treat pelvic floor dysfunction through seminars sponsored by the American Physical Therapy Association, Section on Women's Health.

Kathe Wallace is the co-founder of the Herman and Wallace Pelvic Rehabilitation Institute and to this day continues her mission to educate health care providers and patients on the important and yet poorly understood topic of pelvic floor dysfunction that affects twenty-five percent of US women.

Kathe was honored to receive the Washington State Physical Therapy Association (PTWA) Clinical Excellence Award. She owns a private practice in Seattle, WA, while continuing to lecture nationally and internationally. She serves as a Clinical Instructor, Division of Physical Therapy, Department of Rehabilitation Medicine, at the University of Washington.

www.facebook.com/KatheWallacePT and Author

Made in the USA
San Bernardino, CA
11 June 2020

73214170R00073